# PRACTICAL STEPS TO THINK AND GROW RICH

# PRACTICAL STEPS TO
# THINK
# AND GROW
# RICH
## THE SECRET REVEALED

---

**FORMAT FOR BUSY PEOPLE**

---

*Napoleon Hill*

Edited by Joe Kraynak

Published 2019 by Gildan Media LLC
aka G&D Media
www.GandDmedia.com

PRACTICAL STEPS TO THINK AND GROW RICH. Copyright © 2015 By JMW Group, Inc.

No part of this book may be used, reproduced or transmitted in any manner whatsoever, by any means (electronic, photocopying, recording, or otherwise), without the prior written permission of the author, except in the case of brief quotations embodied in critical articles and reviews. No liability is assumed with respect to the use of the information contained within. Although every precaution has been taken, the author and publisher assume no liability for errors or omissions. Neither is any liability assumed for damages resulting from the use of the information contained herein.

Front Cover design by David Rheinhardt of Pyrographx

Interior design by Meghan Day Healey of Story Horse, LLC

Library of Congress Cataloging-in-Publication Data is available upon request

ISBN: 978-1-7225-0214-0

10   9   8   7   6   5   4   3   2   1

# Contents

Preface to the Current Edition. . . . . . . . . . . . . . . . . . . . . . . . . . . . . . . 7

**Step 1**
Harness the Power of Thought . . . . . . . . . . . . . . . . . . . . . . . . . . . . 13

**Step 2**
Know and Improve Yourself . . . . . . . . . . . . . . . . . . . . . . . . . . . . . .33

**Step 3**
Outwit the Six Ghosts of Fear . . . . . . . . . . . . . . . . . . . . . . . . . . . . 61

**Step 4**
Eliminate Negative Thinking: The Seventh Basic Evil . . . . . . . . . . 81

**Step 5**
Develop a Burning Desire . . . . . . . . . . . . . . . . . . . . . . . . . . . . . . . 99

**Step 6**
Stamp Positive Impressions on Your Subconscious Mind . . . . 129

**Step 7**
Control Your Own Thoughts with Autosuggestion . . . . . . . . . . . 143

**Step 8**
Believe It .................................................... 153

**Step 9**
Engage Your Imagination ................................. 175

**Step 10**
Develop Your Sixth Sense................................. 197

**Step 11**
Crack the Mystery of Sex Transmutation................. 213

**Step 12**
Empower Your Brain: Mental Telepathy and Clairvoyance ....237

**Step 13**
Tap the Power of the Master Mind ........................ 249

**Step 14**
Settle on a Plan ............................................ 265

**Step 15**
Put Specialized Knowledge to Work for You ............... 289

**Step 16**
Be Decisive ................................................. 309

**Step 17**
Be Persistent............................................... 329

# Preface

Success seems to come easy for some people. Without breaking a sweat, they manage to live in luxurious homes, send their children to the best schools, drive fancy cars, travel around the world, and still have resources available to help their loved ones and contribute to the communities in which they live. They are no brighter or better educated than you. They do not work any harder than you do. They do not sacrifice their lives to earn a living; on the contrary, they earn more than enough to fully enjoy their lives.

What is their secret?

Nearly a century ago, world-renowned steel magnate Andrew Carnegie asked this same question and commissioned young journalist Napoleon Hill to answer it. Under the tutelage of Mr. Carnegie, Mr. Hill would spend the next 25 years of his life interviewing over 500 millionaires (and performing 25,000 case studies on those who had failed) in order to unlock the secret formula to success and reveal it to the world. The product of their vision and efforts was the book *Think and Grow Rich*, which has since sold over 15 million copies worldwide, inspired and guided millions of readers and leaders, and helped to shape the world in which we live.

To many people, the idea of sharing the secret of success seemed detrimental. One might think it should remain a carefully guarded secret shared with a select few. But Carnegie and Hill were masters at what they refer to as *Infinite Intelligence*. They knew that the pursuit of wealth and happiness was not a zero-sum endeavor. They knew that wealth and happiness could be created from nothing more than an idea and the desire, intelligence, planning, and perseverance to bring it into being. They knew that increasing wealth and happiness would lead to increasing opportunities that accelerated the growth of wealth and happiness globally. They knew that *sharing the secret would increase opportunities for all men and women*.

In this digital world where people and ideas achieve and lose relevance in an instant, Carnegie's and Hill's not-so-secret formula for success has achieved lasting relevance, because it is rooted in eternal truths and wisdom drawn from nature and human nature. People continue to think and grow rich now as they did so hundreds and even thousands of years ago. *The secret has not changed.* By owning the secret and putting it into practice, you too will attract wealth and happiness beyond what you had ever imagined possible.

Given the enduring success of *Think and Grow Rich* and of the millions of people who have practiced its principles, you may wonder why a revised edition is necessary. Why mess with success? The only reason that warrants a revised edition of any book is this: *To make it better.* In this instance, better does not mean changing the information and concepts that Napoleon

Hill so carefully gathered, analyzed, synthesized, and envisioned. Better means making those concepts and Hill's guidance more accessible to every man and woman.

Napoleon Hill wrote in the style of his day, relying heavily on long and often intricate paragraphs to structure his presentation and weaving practical advice into success stories. Unfortunately, such an approach is more conducive to concealing rather than revealing secrets and limits Carnegie's and Hill's goal of making the secret more accessible to a broader audience. Readers today have neither the time nor the patience to sift through densely packed text to extract essential insights and information. Today's readers also have different backgrounds than did Hill and Carnegie, requiring different examples.

This edition distills the principles presented in *Think and Grow Rich*; presents them in a more easily accessible format, so you do not need to dig through extended paragraphs to mine the nuggets of wisdom; shifts the focus from *what to do* to *how to do it*; enhances the content with additional practical advice; and presents the success stories in a separate section of each chapter, where they serve to illustrate the principles revealed in each step. The words and voice of Napoleon Hill remain in this edition. Although I have restructured some of the paragraphs and updated or omitted some of the examples, the core of this edition's text is Napoleon Hill's book.

Napoleon Hill followers and fans can rest assured that this book remains true to the original and compliments the original book written in 1937. I accepted this commission only after careful consideration and with a commitment to channel the wisdom and spirit Andrew Carnegie and Napoleon Hill into this new edition. Over the course of my career, I have worked with leading experts in a variety of fields to bring their knowledge and wisdom to millions of readers worldwide. This is my first collaboration with deceased experts, but I approach this project with the same reverence toward Mr. Carnegie and Mr. Hill and their collective knowledge and wisdom. Our goal and focus is to remain true to their ideas while revealing the secret to a broader and more modern audience.

Where I diverge from Mr. Hill is in parts of the presentation. While Hill believed that "it (the secret) seems to work more successfully when it is merely uncovered and left in sight, where *those who are ready and searching for it* may pick it up," I believe that revealing the principles as clearly as possible and in a linear, step-by-step fashion makes them more accessible to a broader audience.

You are the only test of whether we have succeeded. As we tell our colleagues and clients, "Your success is our success." If our efforts in this endeavor are successful, they will help you to better understand Mr. Carnegie's and Mr. Hill's formula for success and put it into practice, which will bring you success in all aspects of your life, thus bringing us success in having achieved our goal. We sincerely hope that *our* efforts pay *you* great dividends.

Editor in Chief: Joe Kraynak
JMW GROUP, INC.

*Thought* is a definite idea that combined with purpose, persistence, burning desire, and faith is transmuted into the acquisition of wealth.

The ability to control our thoughts is what enables us to fashion our own reality.

Riches begin with a state of mind, with definiteness of purpose, with little or no hard work.

# Step 1

# Harness the Power of Thought

All accomplishments begin with thought. In fact, you would not be reading this book had you not first thought about reading it. In terms of achieving success, thought is more than a notion or idea. *Thought is the engine of action*. As such, it is more of a *mindset* or *state of mind* than a fleeting notion. It is an idea that combined with purpose, persistence, and a burning desire is transmuted into the acquisition of wealth or any other object of desire. For thought to serve as a sufficient impetus to success, it must be:

- **Definite:** Thought has no contingency plans. It sets its sights on something specific.
- **Purposeful:** The purpose is whatever goal you have in mind, whatever object or situation you desire, whichever direction you choose to move.
- **Persistent:** The "whatever it takes" attitude toward achieving the goal. Few have ever won anything believing they would lose.

- **Burning with desire:** When desire is great enough, no obstacle is insurmountable.
- **Believed:** One must have *faith* and expectation that whatever one desires *will be received*.

---

Thought is energy that drives the action necessary to overcome obstacles between you and that which you desire.

---

## Principles rooted in nature

The principles that enable you to think and grow rich are rooted in nature. You, the earth on which you live, and every other material thing are the result of evolutionary change, through which microscopic bits of matter have been organized and arranged in an orderly fashion. Moreover, this earth, every one of the billions of individual cells of your body, and every atom of matter, *began as an intangible form of energy.*

*Desire* is thought impulse! Thought impulses are forms of energy. When you begin with the thought impulse, the *desire* to accumulate money, you are drafting into your service the same "stuff" that nature used in creating this earth and every material form in the universe, including the body and brain in which the thought impulses originate.

As far as science has been able to determine, the entire universe consists of matter and energy. The combination of energy and matter has created everything perceptible from the largest star that floats in the heavens down to the tiniest grain of sand.

You are now engaged in the task of trying to profit by nature's method. You are (sincerely and earnestly, we hope) trying to adapt yourself to nature's laws by endeavoring to convert *desire* into its physical and monetary equivalent. *You can do it! It has been done before!*

You can build a fortune through the aid of laws that are immutable. But first, you must become familiar with these laws and learn to *use* them. Through repetition and by approaching the description of these principles from every conceivable angle, the author hopes to reveal to you the secret through which great fortunes has been accumulated. Strange and paradoxical as it may seem, the "secret" is *not a secret*. Nature, herself, advertises it on the earth on which we live, the stars, the planets suspended within our view, in the elements above and around us, in every blade of grass, and in every form of life within our vision.

Nature advertises this "secret" in the terms of biology, in the conversion of a tiny cell, so small that it may be lost on the point of a pin, into the *human being* now reading this line. The conversion of desire into its physical equivalent is certainly no more miraculous!

Do not become discouraged if you do not fully comprehend all that has been stated. Unless you have long been a student of the mind, it is not to be expected that you will assimilate all that is in this chapter upon a first reading.

But you will, in time, make good progress.

The principles that follow will open the way for understanding of imagination. Assimilate that which you understand, as you read this philosophy for the first time, then, when you reread and study it, you will discover that something has happened to clarify it and give you a broader understanding of the whole. Above all, *do not stop*, nor hesitate in your study of these principles until you have read the book at least *three* times, for then you will not want to stop.

## You are "The Master of Your Fate, The Captain of Your Soul"

When, the English poet, W.C. Henley wrote the prophetic lines, "I am the Master of my Fate, I am the Captain of my Soul," he should have informed us of the reason we are the Masters of our Fate, the Captains of our Souls: that we have the power to control our *thoughts* and that our *thoughts shape our reality*. Here is how thought shapes reality:

- The ether in which this little earth floats, in which we move and have our being, is a form of energy moving at an inconceivably high rate of vibration. This ether is filled with a form of universal power which *adapts* itself to the nature of the thoughts we hold in our minds and *influences* us, in natural ways, to transmute our thoughts into their physical equivalent.
- This power makes no attempt to discriminate between destructive thoughts and constructive thoughts. It will translate into physical reality thoughts of poverty just as quickly as it will translate into physical reality thoughts of riches.
- Our brains become magnetized with the dominating thoughts which we hold in our minds, and, by means with which no person is familiar, these "magnets" attract to us the forces, the people, the circumstances of life which harmonize with the nature of our dominating thoughts.
- Before we can accumulate riches in great abundance, we must magnetize our minds with intense *desire* for riches. We must become "money conscious" until the

*desire* for money becomes a sufficient force to transmute desire into wealth.

*You truly are the Master of Your Fate, the Captain of Your Soul.* This natural and enduring truth is at the root of the principles described in this book, the principles that unlock the secret of gaining mastery over your financial fate.

## Develop success consciousness

The Great Depression started in 1929, and continued on to an all-time record of destruction, until sometime after President Franklin D. Roosevelt entered office. Then the depression began to fade into nothingness. Just as an electrician in a theatre raises the lights so gradually that darkness is transmuted into light before you realize it, so did the spell of fear in the minds of the people gradually fade away as faith filled the darkness. Through the power of thought, what seemed impossible became possible.

Some who will read this book will believe that no one can *think and grow rich*. They cannot think in terms of riches, because their thought habits have been steeped in poverty, want, misery, failure, and defeat. To think and grow rich, the first step is to adopt the proper mindset:

- **Become *success conscious*.** Success comes to those who become *success conscious*. Failure comes to those who indifferently allow themselves to become *failure conscious*.
- **Stop thinking in terms of *impossible and cannot*.** People readily point out proposed solutions that will *not*

work and *cannot* be done. Purge these and other self-defeating words from your vocabulary.

- **Gauge opportunity by what is possible, not by your own impressions and beliefs.** People tend to develop a habit of measuring everything and everyone by their own self-limiting impressions and beliefs. Don't let preconceptions hold you or others back from achieving what is possible.

---

The object of this book is to help all who seek it learn the art of changing their minds from *failure consciousness* to *success consciousness*.

---

## Stories that illustrate the power of thought

The stories that follow demonstrate how intangible thought combined with purpose, persistence, and a burning desire translates into the acquisition of tangible wealth and how the power to control one's thoughts shape one's reality.

### The man who thought his way into partnership with Thomas A. Edison

Edwin C. Barnes harnessed the power of thought to become a business partner of the great Thomas Edison. Two of the chief characteristics of Barnes' thought were that it was *definite* and *purposeful*: He wanted to work *with* Edison, not *for* him.

Two difficulties stood in Barnes' way: He did not know Mr. Edison and did not have the means to travel to Orange, New Jersey to meet him. These difficulties were sufficient to have discouraged the majority of people, but his was no ordinary thought! It was coupled with *persistence* and *burning desire*. Barnes was so determined to find a way to achieve his goal that he finally decided to travel by "blind baggage" (via freight train).

He presented himself at Mr. Edison's laboratory and announced that he had come to go into business with the inventor. In speaking of the first meeting between Barnes and Edison, years later, Mr. Edison said:

He stood there before me, looking like an ordinary tramp, but there was something in the expression of his face which conveyed the impression that he was determined to get what he had come after. I had learned, from years of experience with men, that when a man really *desires* a thing so deeply that he is willing to stake his entire future on a single turn of the wheel in order to get it, he is sure to win. I gave him the opportunity he asked for, because I saw he had made up his mind to stand by until he succeeded. Subsequent events proved that no mistake was made.

Just what young Barnes said to Mr. Edison on that occasion was far less important than that which he *thought*. Edison, himself, said so! It could not have been the young man's appearance that got him his start in the Edison office, for that was definitely against him. It was what he *thought* that counted.

---

It wasn't the Barnes' appearance that got him his start in Edison's office. It was what he *thought* that counted.

---

Barnes did not get his partnership with Edison immediately. He did get a chance to work in the Edison offices, at a very nominal wage, doing work that was unimportant to Edison, but most important to Barnes, because it gave him an opportunity to prove himself.

Months went by. Apparently nothing happened to bring the coveted goal, which Barnes had set up in his mind as his *definite major purpose*. But something important was happening in Barnes' mind. He was constantly intensifying his *desire* to become the business associate of Edison.

Psychologists have correctly said, "When one is truly ready for a thing, it puts in its appearance." Barnes was ready for a business association with Edison; moreover, he was *determined to remain ready until he got that which he was seeking.*

He did not say to himself, "Ah well, what's the use? I guess I'll change my mind and try for a salesman's job." But, he did say, "I came here to go into business with Edison, and I'll accomplish this end if it takes the remainder of my life." He meant it! What a different story people would have to tell if only they would adopt a definite purpose and stand by that purpose until it had time to become an all-consuming obsession!

---

"When one is truly ready for a thing, it puts in its appearance."

---

Maybe young Barnes did not know it at the time, but his bulldog determination, his persistence in pursuing a single *desire*, was destined to mow down all opposition and bring him the opportunity he was seeking.

When the opportunity came, it appeared in a different form and from a different direction than Barnes had expected. That is one of the tricks of opportunity. It has a sly habit of slipping in by the back door, and often it comes disguised in the form of misfortune, or temporary defeat. Perhaps this is why so many fail to recognize opportunity.

Mr. Edison had just perfected a new office device, known at that time, as the Edison Dictating Machine (later called the Idiophone). His sales people were not enthusiastic over the machine. They did not believe it could be sold without great effort. Barnes saw his opportunity. It had crawled in quietly, hidden in a queer looking machine that interested no one but Barnes and the inventor.

Barnes *knew* (*definite purpose* fueled by *persistence* and *burning desire*) that he could sell the Edison Dictating Machine. He suggested this to Edison and promptly got his chance. He did sell the machine. In fact, he sold it so successfully that Edison gave him a contract to distribute and market it all over the nation. Out of that business association grew the slogan, "Made by Edison and installed by Barnes." Out of this business alliance Barnes made himself wealthy, but he accomplished something infinitely greater, he proved that one really may *think and grow rich*.

Barnes literally *thought* himself into a partnership with the great Edison! He *thought* himself into a fortune. He had nothing to start with, no money or influence, and little education. But he did have initiative, faith, and the will to win. He *knew what he wanted and was determined to stand by that desire until he realized it*. With these intangible forces he made himself number one man with the greatest inventor who ever lived.

---

Barnes literally *thought* himself into a partnership with the great Edison!

---

Now, let us look at a different situation, and study a man who had plenty of tangible evidence of riches but lost it, because he stopped three feet short of his goal.

## Quitting three feet from gold

One of the most common causes of failure is the habit of quitting when one is overtaken by temporary defeat. Every person is guilty of this mistake at one time or another. This is a story of how thought without persistence can lead to failure.

R. U. Darby, who later became one of the most successful insurance salesmen in the country, tells the story of his uncle, who was caught by the "gold fever" in the gold-rush days and went west to *dig and grow rich*. He had never heard that more gold has been mined from the brains of men than has ever been taken from the earth. He staked a claim and went to work with pick and shovel. His thought was certainly *definite*, *purposeful*, and driven by a *burning desire*, a lust for gold.

---

Thought without persistence often leads to failure.

---

After weeks of labor, he was rewarded by the discovery of the shining ore. He needed machinery to bring the ore to the surface. Quietly, he covered up the mine, retraced his footsteps to his home in Williamsburg, Maryland, and told his relatives and a few neighbors of the "strike." They got together money for the needed machinery and had it shipped. The uncle and Darby went back to work the mine.

The first car of ore was mined and shipped to a smelter. The returns proved they had one of the richest mines in Colorado!

A few more cars of that ore would clear the debts. Then would come the big killing in profits.

Down went the drills! Up went the hopes of Darby and his uncle! Then something happened! The vein of gold ore disappeared! They had come to the end of the rainbow, and the pot of gold was nowhere to be found! They drilled on, desperately trying to pick up the vein all to no avail.

Finally, they decided to *quit*. They sold the machinery to a junk man for a few hundred dollars and took the train back home. Some junk men are dumb, but not this one! He called in a mining engineer to look at the mine and do a little calculating. The engineer advised that the project had failed, because the owners were unfamiliar with "fault lines." His calculations showed that the vein would be found *just three feet from where the Darbys had stopped drilling*! That is exactly where it was found! The junk man took millions of dollars in ore from the mine, because he knew enough to seek expert counsel before giving up.

---

The junk man had no *specialized knowledge* about fault lines, but he had the wisdom to hire someone who did. See Step 15 for more about how to harness the power of specialized knowledge when you are not in possession of it yourself.

---

Long afterward, Mr. Darby recouped his loss many times over, when he made the discovery that *desire* can be transmuted into gold. The discovery came after he went into the business of selling life insurance.

Remembering that he lost a huge fortune, because he had *stopped* three feet from gold, Darby profited by the experience in his chosen work, by the simple method of saying to himself,

"I stopped three feet from gold, but I will never stop because men say 'no' when I ask them to buy insurance." He owes his stick-to-itiveness to the lesson he learned from quitting short of achieving his goal in the gold mining business.

---

> Before success comes to most people, they are sure to meet with much temporary defeat and, perhaps, some failure. When faced with defeat, the easiest and most logical thing to do is to *quit*. Persistence is the key to succeeding in the face of adversity.

---

More than five hundred of the most successful people this country has ever known claim that their greatest success came just one step beyond the point at which defeat had overtaken them. Failure is a trickster with a keen sense of irony and cunning. It takes great delight in tripping one when success is almost within reach.

*Persistence* is key in foiling failure, as our next story demonstrates.

### A fifty cent lesson in persistence

Shortly after Mr. Darby received his degree from the "University of Hard Knocks" and learned the painful lesson of persistence, he had the good fortune to be present on an occasion that proved to him that "no" does not necessarily mean no.

One afternoon he was helping his uncle grind wheat in an old fashioned mill. The uncle operated a large farm on which a number of sharecrop farmers lived. Quietly, the door was opened, and a small child, the daughter of a tenant, walked in and took her place near the door.

The uncle looked up, saw the child, and barked at her roughly, "What do you want?"

Meekly, the child replied, "My mammy says send her fifty cents."

"I'll not do it," the uncle retorted, "Now you run on home."

"Yes, sir," the child replied. But she did not move.

The uncle went ahead with his work, so busily engaged that he did not pay enough attention to the child to observe that she did not leave. When he looked up and saw her still standing there, he yelled at her, "I told you to go on home! Now go, or I'll take a switch to you."

The little girl said, "Yes, sir," but she did not budge an inch.

The uncle dropped a sack of grain he was about to pour into the mill hopper, picked up a barrel stave, and started toward the child with an expression on his face that indicated trouble.

Darby held his breath. He was certain he was about to witness a murder. He knew his uncle had a fierce temper. When the uncle reached the spot where the child was standing, she quickly stepped forward one step, looked up into his eyes, and screamed at the top of her shrill voice, *"My mammy's gotta have that fifty cents!"*

The uncle stopped, looked at her for a minute, then slowly laid the barrel stave on the floor, put his hand in his pocket, took out half a dollar, and gave it to her.

The child took the money and slowly backed toward the door, never taking her eyes off the man whom she had just conquered. After she had gone, the uncle sat down on a box and looked out the window into space for more than ten minutes. He was pondering, with awe, over the whipping he had just taken.

Mr. Darby, too, was doing some thinking. That was the first time in all his experience that he had seen the child of a sharecropper deliberately master an adult authority figure. How did she do it? What happened to his uncle that caused him to lose his fierceness and become as docile as a lamb? What strange power did this child use that made her master over her superior? These and other similar questions flashed into Darby's mind, but he did not find the answer until years later, when he told me the story.

Strangely, the story of this unusual experience was told to me in the old mill, on the very spot where the uncle took his whipping.

As we stood there in that musty old mill, Mr. Darby repeated the story of the unusual conquest and finished by asking, "What can you make of it? What strange power did that child use, that so completely whipped my uncle?"

After I had described to Mr. Darby the power unwittingly used by the little child, the power of *thought*, as described at the beginning of this chapter, he quickly retraced his thirty years of experience as a life insurance salesman, and frankly acknowledged that his success in that field was due, in no small degree, to the lesson he had learned from the child.

Mr. Darby pointed out: "Every time a prospect tried to bow me out, without buying, I saw that child standing there in the old mill, her big eyes glaring in defiance, and I said to myself, 'I've gotta make this sale.' The better portion of all sales I have made, were made after people had said 'no'."

He recalled, too, the mistake he and his uncle made stopping only three feet from gold, "But," he said, "that experience was a blessing in disguise. It taught me to keep on keeping on, no matter how hard the going may be, a lesson I needed to learn before I could succeed in anything." Darby owes to these two experiences his ability to sell more than a million dollars of life insurance every year.

## Henry Ford and his V-8 engine

Millions of people have noted the achievements of Henry Ford and envied him because of his good fortune or luck or genius or whatever it is that they credited for Ford's fortune. Perhaps one person in every hundred thousand knows the secret of Ford's success, and those who do know are too modest or too reluctant to speak of it, because of its simplicity. A single incident will illustrate *the secret* perfectly.

When Ford decided to produce his now famous V-8 motor, he chose to build an engine with the entire eight cylinders cast in one block and instructed his engineers to produce a design for the engine. The design was placed on paper, but the engineers believed that it was impossible to cast an eight cylinder gas engine block in one piece.

Ford said, "Produce it anyway."

"But," they replied, "it's impossible!"

"Go ahead," Ford commanded, "and stay on the job until you succeed no matter how much time is required."

The engineers went ahead. There was nothing else for them to do if they were to remain on the Ford staff. Six months went by, and nothing happened. Another six months passed, and still nothing happened. The engineers tried every conceivable plan to carry out the orders, but the thing seemed out of the question, "Impossible!"

At the end of the year Ford checked with his engineers, and again they informed him they had found no way to carry out his orders.

"Go right ahead," said Ford, "I want it, and I'll have it."

They went ahead, and then, as if by a stroke of magic, the secret was discovered. The Ford *determination* had won once more!

---

Henry Ford became a success, because he understood and applied the principles of success. One of these is *desire*: knowing what one wanted. The other is *persistence*: persevering until the object of desire was obtained. Remember this Ford story as you read, because it reveals *the secret*, the principles by which any object of desire is obtained.

---

### From milkshakes to McDonald's with Ray Kroc

Ray Kroc is a good example of another person whose riches originated with a *thought*. Kroc was a salesman of milk-shake mixers. Most of his customers—restaurants and diners—purchased one or two units. When he received an order for eight mixers from a small food outlet in San Bernadino, California, he decided to visit them and see how they could sell so many shakes. It was the busiest restaurant he had ever seen. The brothers offered a very limited menu: hamburgers, cheeseburgers, French fries, shakes, and soft drinks, all at the lowest prices in the area.

Kroc saw an opportunity. If he could open a chain of these restaurants, each as productive and profitable as this, money would flow in. He proposed the idea to the McDonald brothers, who teamed up with Kroc to implement it. Within a few years, McDonald's not only became the top selling food outlet in the country, but launched the fast-food industry. Kroc later bought out the McDonald brothers and expanded the business into an international phenomenon, making him one of the richest men of his time.

---

> McDonald's started with a *thought*—to offer a limited menu at the lowest prices in the area. It grew into a world-wide billion dollar, fast-food franchise from another *thought*—to create a chain of these fast food restaurants. Both thoughts were intangibles that ultimately produced tangible wealth.

---

## About this book

Most people who sincerely desire to improve themselves and their station in life yearn to know the secret to *how people become wealthy*. Many wealthy people have learned these important life lessons on their own, just as Darby did by observing his and his uncle's mistake of stopping three feet short of gold and from the 50-cent lesson in persistence. Few others, however, have the good fortune of observing such valuable life lessons or the ability to extract insight from such lessons. I wrote this book to make *the secret* more accessible to more people.

---

> Riches begin with a state of mind, with definiteness of purpose, with little or no hard work.

I spent twenty-five years in research, interviewing more than 500 wealthy individuals and analyzing more than 25,000 people who failed at their efforts to become rich, because I, too, wanted to know *how wealthy people became rich*. Without that research, this book could not have been written.

As you proceed, remember this: Riches begin with a state of mind, with definiteness of purpose, with little or no hard work. In this book, you learn how to acquire that state of mind which will attract riches. When you begin to think and grow rich, you soon discover the following:

When riches begin to come they come so quickly, in such great abundance, that one wonders where they have been hiding during all those lean years.

This is an astounding statement, and all the more so, when we take into consideration the popular misconception that riches come only to those who work hard and long.

You may see your best friend and your greatest enemy by stepping in front of a mirror.

# Step 2

# Know and Improve Yourself

The oldest of admonitions is "Know thyself!" To be successful in any pursuit, you must know yourself, your strengths and weaknesses, and continually strive to improve your strengths and eliminate weaknesses. The most common cause of both success and failure is *self*. Any weakness in one's self works to undermine success. Here, I encourage you and show you how to evaluate yourself, and I present a list of 31 common obstacles to success, so you can begin to work toward removing them from your path.

---

The most common cause of both success and failure is *self*.

---

## Choose to lead or follow

Before deciding on a specific approach to accumulating riches, you must decide whether to pursue riches as a leader or a follower:

- *Leaders* accumulate riches by creating opportunities and inducing followers to design, produce, market, and distribute products and services to the marketplace.
- *Followers* may accumulate riches by selling their specialized knowledge in the form of services to leaders.

It is no disgrace to be a follower. On the other hand, it is no credit to remain a follower. Most great leaders began in the capacity of followers. They became great leaders because they were *intelligent followers*. With few exceptions, people who cannot follow a leader intelligently cannot become efficient leaders. People who can follow a leader most efficiently are usually those who develop into leadership most rapidly. An intelligent follower has many advantages, among them the *opportunity to acquire knowledge from the leader.*

---

The difference in compensation is vast. The follower cannot reasonably expect the compensation to which a leader is entitled, although many followers make the mistake of expecting such pay.

---

### Recognize the major leadership attributes

If you choose to pursue riches as a leader, be sure you possess the following 11 essential leadership attributes:

1. **Unwavering courage** based upon knowledge of self, and of one's occupation: No follower wishes to be dominated by a leader who lacks self-confidence and courage. No intelligent follower will be dominated by such a leader very long.

2. **Self-control:** People, who cannot control themselves, can never control others. Self-control sets a mighty example for one's followers, which the more intelligent will emulate.
3. **Keen sense of justice:** Without a sense of fairness and justice, no leader can command and retain the respect of his or her followers.
4. **Definiteness of decision:** People who waver in decisions show that they are unsure of themselves. They cannot lead others successfully.
5. **Definiteness of plans:** The successful leader must plan the work and work the plan. A leader who moves by guesswork, without practical, definite plans, is comparable to a ship without a rudder. Sooner or later it will land on the rocks.
6. **Habit of doing more than one is paid for:** Leaders must do more than they require of their followers.
7. **Pleasing personality:** No slovenly, careless person can become a successful leader. Leadership calls for respect. Followers will not respect leaders who do not have a pleasing personality, sometimes referred to as charisma.
8. **Sympathy and understanding:** Successful leaders must be in sympathy with their followers. Moreover, they must understand them and their problems.
9. **Mastery of detail:** Successful leadership calls for mastery of details of the leader's position.
10. **Willingness to assume full responsibility:** Successful leaders must be willing to assume responsibility for the mistakes and the shortcomings of their followers. If they try to shift this responsibility, they will not remain leaders.

If followers make mistakes and become incompetent, it is the leader who has failed.

11. **Cooperation:** Successful leaders must understand and apply the principle of cooperative effort and be able to induce followers to do the same. Leadership calls for *power*, and power calls for *cooperation*.

## Note the ten major causes of failure in leadership

Knowing *what not to do* is as important as knowing what *to do*. Here are the ten major causes of leadership failure:

1. **Inability to organize details:** Efficient leadership calls for ability to organize and to master details. No genuine leader is ever too busy to do anything that may be required as a leader. Whether a leader or follower is too busy to change plans or attend to any emergency, it is an indication of inefficiency. The successful leader must be the master of all details connected with the position. That means, of course, that the leader must be able to delegate responsibilities effectively.

2. **Unwillingness to render humble service:** Truly great leaders are willing, when occasion demands, to perform any sort of labor that they would ask another to perform. "The greatest among ye shall be the servant of all" is a truth that all able leaders observe and respect.

3. **Expectation of pay for what they "know" instead of what they do with that which they know:** The world does not pay for that which people "know." It pays them for what they *do* or induce others to do.

4. **Fear of competition from followers:** The leader who fears that one of his followers may take his position is practically

sure to realize that fear sooner or later. Able leaders train understudies to whom they may delegate at will. Only in this way may leaders multiply themselves and prepare to be at many places and give attention to many things at one time. It is an eternal truth that people receive more pay for their ability to get others to perform than they could possibly earn by their own efforts. Efficient leaders may, through knowledge of their jobs and the magnetism of their personalities, greatly increase the efficiency of others and induce them to render more and better service than they could render by themselves.

5. **Lack of imagination:** Without imagination, leaders are incapable of meeting emergencies and creating plans by which to guide followers efficiently.
6. **Selfishness:** Leaders who claim all of the honor for the work of their followers are sure to encounter resentment. Great leaders claim none of the honors. They are content to see the honors, when there are any, go to their followers, because they know that most people will work harder for commendation and recognition than they will for money alone.
7. **Intemperance:** Followers do not respect an intemperate leader. Moreover, intemperance in any of its various forms destroys the endurance and the vitality of all who indulge in it.
8. **Disloyalty:** Perhaps this should have come at the top of the list. Leaders who are not loyal to their trust and to their associates (those above and below them) cannot long maintain their leadership. Disloyalty marks one as being less than the dust of the earth and brings down on one's

head well-deserved contempt. Lack of loyalty is one of the major causes of failure in every walk of life.

9. **Emphasis of the "authority" of leadership:** Efficient leaders lead by encouraging and not by trying to instill fear in the hearts of their followers. Leaders who try to impress followers with their "authority" come within the category of leadership through force. Real leaders have no need to advertise that fact except by their conduct, sympathy, understanding, fairness, and a demonstration of knowledge of the job.
10. **Emphasis of title:** Competent leaders require no "title" to gain the respect of their followers. Leaders who make too much over the title generally have little else to emphasize. The doors to the office of real leaders are open to all who wish to enter, and their working quarters are free from formality or ostentation.

These are among the more common of the causes of failure in leadership. Any one of these faults is sufficient to induce failure. Study the list carefully if you aspire to leadership, and be free of these faults.

### Explore fertile fields for new leadership

Leadership opportunities abound in all fields, because leaders create and identify opportunities that add value. Here are several fertile fields that have experienced a decline in leadership and in which the new type of leader may find an abundance of *opportunity*:

- **Politics:** The demand for competent politicians with integrity is nothing less than an emergency. Too many politicians have seemingly become high-grade, legalized racketeers. They have increased taxes and debauched the machinery of industry and business until the people can no longer stand the burden.

- **Finance and economics:** Chronic global instability in the financial markets has all but destroyed public confidence. The world needs leaders who understand and appreciate the financial principles on which stable economic systems are based and have the moral integrity to do the right thing instead of enabling financial institutions to reap short-term profits at the expense of the health of the system.
- **Business:** The old type of leaders thought and moved in terms of dividends instead of in terms of human equations! Exploitation of workers and collective bargaining that puts companies out of business are, or at least should be, a thing of the past. Let those who aspire to leadership in the field of business, industry, and labor remember this.
- **Religion:** Religious leaders of the future will be forced to give more attention to the current needs of their followers, especially in terms of personal finance and relationships, and less attention to the dead past and yet unborn future.
- **Professions:** In the professions of law, medicine, and education, a new brand of leadership, and to some extent, new leaders will become a necessity. This is especially true in the field of education, where educators must find ways and means to teach people *how to apply* the knowledge they receive in school. They must deal more with *practice* and less with *theory*.

- **Media:** The media (newspapers, magazines, movies, television, games, websites, radio, and so on) mold the minds that plot the course of future civilization. Wise, unbiased leaders are needed to make responsible use of these powerful tools to ensure positive change.

These are but a few of the fields in which opportunities for new leaders and a new brand of leadership are now available.

---

A *leader* is one who creates opportunities and induces followers to design, produce, market, and distribute products and services to the marketplace.

---

### Know the importance of leadership by consent

There are two forms of leadership:
- **Leadership by consent** of and with the sympathy of the followers is by far the most effective.
- **Leadership by force**, without the consent and sympathy of the followers, is unsustainable.

History is filled with evidence that leadership by force cannot endure. The downfall and disappearance of dictators and kings is significant. It means that people will not follow forced leadership indefinitely. The world has entered a new era of relationship between leaders and followers, which very clearly calls for new leaders and a new brand of leadership in business and industry. Those who belong to the old school of leadership by force must acquire an understanding of the new brand of leadership (cooperation) or be relegated to the rank and file of the followers. There is no other way out for them.

The relationship of employer and employee, or of leader and follower, in the future, will be one of mutual cooperation based upon an equitable division of the profits of business. In the future, the relationship of employer and employee will be more like a partnership than it has been in the past. Hitler, Stalin, and Saddam Hussein are examples of leadership by force. Their leadership passed. Without much difficulty, one might point to the prototypes of these ex-leaders, among the business, financial, and labor leaders of America who have been dethroned or slated to go. *Leadership by consent* of the followers is the only brand that can endure!

---

Leadership by force cannot endure.
People may follow the forced leadership temporarily,
but they will not do so willingly or for long.

---

The new brand of *leadership* will embrace the eleven essential leadership attributes, described in this chapter, as well as some other attributes. People who make these the basis of their leadership will find abundant opportunity to lead in any walk of life.

## Remove obstacles to success: The 31 major causes of failure

Life's greatest tragedy lies in the overwhelmingly large majority of people who earnestly try and fail, as compared to the few who succeed.

I have had the privilege of analyzing several thousand men and women, 98% of whom were classed as failures. There is something radically wrong with a civilization and a system of education that permit 98% of the people to go through life as failures. But I did not write this book for the purpose of moralizing on the rights and wrongs of the world; that would require a book a hundred times the size of this one.

---

You may see at one and the same time both your best friend and your greatest enemy by stepping in front of a mirror.

---

My analysis proved that there are at least 31 major reasons for failure and 17 steps people take to accumulate fortunes. Below is a list of the 31 major causes of failure plus an open category for any other excuse one can think up for not being successful. As you go over the list, check yourself by it, point by point, for the purpose of discovering how many of these causes of failure stand between you and success.

1. **Unfavorable hereditary background**: There is but little, if anything, that can be done for people who are born with a deficiency in brainpower. This philosophy offers but one method of bridging this weakness—through the aid of the *Master Mind*. Observe with profit, however, that this is the *only* one of the thirty causes of failure that may not be easily corrected by any individual.
2. **Lack of a well-defined purpose in life:** There is no hope of success for the person who does not have a central purpose, or definite goal at which to aim. Ninety-eight out of every one hundred of those whom I have analyzed had no such aim. Perhaps this was the *major cause of their failure*.

3. **Lack of ambition to aim above mediocrity:** We offer no hope for the person who is so indifferent as not to want to get ahead in life and who is not willing to pay the price.
4. **Insufficient education:** This is a handicap that may be overcome with comparative ease. Experience has proven that the best-educated people are often those who are known as "self-made" or self-educated. It takes more than a college degree to make one a person of education. Any person who is educated is one who has learned to get whatever he or she wants in life without violating the rights of others. Education consists not so much of knowledge but of knowledge effectively and persistently *applied*. People are paid, not merely for what they know, but more particularly for *what they do with that which they know.*
5. **Lack of self-discipline:** Discipline comes through self-control. This means that one must control all negative qualities. Before you can control conditions, you must first control yourself. Self-mastery is the hardest job you will ever tackle. If you do not conquer self, you will be conquered by self. You may see at one and the same time both your best friend and your greatest enemy by stepping in front of a mirror.
6. **Ill health:** No person may enjoy outstanding success without good health. Many of the causes of ill health are subject to mastery and control. These, in the main are:
    + Overconsumption of foods not conducive to health
        + Overindulgence in harmful substances, such as nicotine and alcohol
    + Wrong habits of thought; giving expression to negatives
    + Wrong use of, and over indulgence in sex

- Lack of proper physical exercise
- An inadequate supply of fresh air, due to improper breathing

7. **Unfavorable environmental influences during childhood:** "As the twig is bent, so shall the tree grow." Most people who have criminal tendencies acquire them as the result of bad environment and improper associates during childhood.

8. **Procrastination:** This is one of the most common causes of failure. "Old Man Procrastination" stands within the shadow of all people, waiting their opportunity to spoil their chances of success. Most of us go through life as failures, because we are waiting for the "time to be right" to start doing something worthwhile. Do not wait. The time will never be "just right." Start where you stand and work with whatever tools you may have at your command; better tools will be found as you go along.

9. **Lack of persistence:** Most of us are good "starters" but poor "finishers" of everything we begin. Moreover, people are prone to give up at the first signs of defeat. There is no substitute for *persistence*. The *persistent* person discovers that "Old Man Failure" finally becomes tired and *goes away*. Failure cannot cope with *persistence*.

10. **Negative personality:** There is no hope of success for the person who repels people through a negative personality. Success comes through the application of *power*, and power is attained through the cooperative efforts of other people. A negative personality will not induce cooperation.

11. **Lack of controlled sexual urge:** Sex energy is the most powerful of all the stimuli that move people into *action*.

Because it is the most powerful of the emotions, it must be controlled, through transmutation, and converted into other channels.

12. **Uncontrolled desire for "something for nothing:"** The gambling instinct drives millions of people to failure. Evidence of this may be found in a study of the dot.com fiasco of the early 2000s, during which millions of people tried to make money by investing in fly-by-night companies.
13. **Lack of a well-defined power of decision:** People who succeed reach decisions promptly and change them, if at all, very slowly. People who fail, reach decisions, if at all, very slowly and change them frequently and quickly. Indecision and procrastination are twins. Where one is found, the other may usually be found also. Kill off this pair before they completely "hog-tie" you to the treadmill of *failure*.
14. **One or more of the six basic fears:** These fears have been analyzed for you in Step 3. They must be mastered before you can market your services effectively.
15. **Wrong selection of a mate in marriage:** This is a most common cause of failure. The relationship of marriage brings people intimately into contact. Unless this relationship is harmonious, failure is likely to follow. Moreover, it will be a form of failure that is marked by misery and unhappiness, destroying all signs of *ambition*.
16. **Over-caution:** The person, who takes no chances generally has to take whatever is left when others are through choosing. Over-caution is as bad as under-caution. Both are extremes to be guarded against. Life itself is filled with the element of chance.

17. **Wrong selection of associates in business:** This is one of the most common causes of failure in business. In marketing personal services, one should use great care to select an employer who will be an inspiration and who is intelligent and successful. We emulate those with whom we associate most closely. Pick an employer who is worth emulating.

18. **Superstition and prejudice:** Superstition is a form of fear. It is also a sign of ignorance. People who succeed keep open minds and are afraid of nothing.

19. **Wrong selection of a vocation:** No one can succeed in a line of endeavor which he or she does not like. The most essential step in the marketing of personal services is that of selecting an occupation into which you can throw yourself wholeheartedly.

20. **Lack of concentration of effort:** The "jack-of-all-trades" seldom is good at any. Concentrate all of your efforts on one *definite chief aim*.

21. **The habit of indiscriminate spending:** Spendthrifts cannot succeed, mainly because they stand eternally in *fear of poverty*. Form the habit of systematic saving by putting aside a definite percentage of your income. Money in the bank gives one a very safe foundation of *courage* when bargaining for the sale of personal services. Without money, one must take what one is offered and be glad to get it.

22. **Lack of enthusiasm:** Without enthusiasm one cannot be convincing. Moreover, enthusiasm is contagious, and the person who has it under control is generally welcome in any group of people.

23. **Intolerance:** The person with a "closed" mind on any subject seldom gets ahead. Intolerance means that one has

stopped acquiring knowledge. The most damaging forms of intolerance are those connected with religious, racial, and political differences of opinion.
24. **Intemperance:** The most damaging forms of intemperance are connected with eating, strong drink, and sexual activities. Overindulgence in any of these is fatal to success.
25. **Inability to cooperate with others:** More people lose their positions and their big opportunities in life because of this fault than for all other reasons combined. It is a fault that no well-informed business executive or leader will tolerate.
26. **Possession of power that was not acquired through self-effort:** (This applies to sons and daughters of wealthy families and others who inherit money that they did not earn). Power in the hands of one who did not acquire it gradually is often fatal to success. *Quick riches* are more dangerous than poverty.
27. **Intentional dishonesty:** There is no substitute for honesty. One may be temporarily dishonest by force of circumstances over which one has no control, without permanent damage. But, there is *no* HOPE for people who are dishonest by choice. Sooner or later, their deeds will catch up with them, and they will pay by loss of reputation and perhaps even loss of liberty.
28. **Egotism and vanity:** These qualities serve as red lights that warn others to keep away. *They are fatal to success.*
29. **Guessing instead of thinking:** Most people are too indifferent or lazy to acquire *facts* with which to *think accurately*. They prefer to act on "opinions" created by guesswork or snap-judgments.

30. **Lack of capital:** This is a common cause of failure among those who start out in business for the first time, without sufficient reserve of capital to absorb the shock of their mistakes, and to carry them over until they have established a *reputation*.
31. **Other:** Under this, name any particular cause of failure from which you have suffered that has not been included in the foregoing list.

---

**Tip:** Evaluate yourself in terms of these 31 common causes of failure, then ask one or more other people to evaluate you—perhaps a supervisor, a friend, a teacher, a colleague, and a client. Having several different perspectives provides a more complete and objective view of your strengths and weaknesses.

---

## Appreciate the opportunities and resources you have

One major obstacle to success not named specifically in the previous section is the making of excuses, which could be attributed to every single item in the list. Part of self-knowledge and self-improvement involves recognizing when you are making excuses and, hence, placing limitations on your own success and adjusting your attitude to more fully appreciate the advantages you have, especially if you are living in a country with a free-market (capitalist) economy, such as the United States of America. Let us take inventory of what the United States of America offers the person seeking riches, great or small.

To begin with, let us remember, all of us, that we live in a country where every law-abiding citizen enjoys freedom of thought and freedom of deed unequaled anywhere in the world. Most of us have never taken inventory of the advantages of this freedom. We have never compared our unlimited freedom with the curtailed freedom in other countries.

Here we have freedom of thought; freedom in the choice and enjoyment of education; freedom in religion; freedom in politics; freedom in the choice of a business, profession, or occupation; freedom to accumulate and own without molestation *all the property we can accumulate*; freedom to choose our place of residence; freedom in marriage; freedom through equal opportunity to all races; freedom of travel from one state to another; freedom in our choice of foods; and freedom to *aim for any station in life for which we have prepared ourselves*, even for the presidency of the United States.

We have other forms of freedom, but this list gives a bird's eye view of the most important, which constitute *opportunity* of the highest order. This advantage of freedom is all the more conspicuous because the United States is the only country guaranteeing to every citizen, whether native born or naturalized, so broad and varied a list of freedoms.

Next, let us recount some of the blessings that our widespread freedom has placed within our hands. Look at the average American family (meaning, the family of average income) and sum up the benefits available to every member of the family in this land of *opportunity* and plenty! Next to freedom of thought and deed come *food, clothing,* and *shelter,* the three basic necessities of life:

- **Food:** Because of our universal freedom the average American family has available, at its very door, the choicest selection of food to be found anywhere in the world, and at prices within its financial range.
- **Clothing:** Anywhere in the United States, men and women can meet their clothing requirements and dress very comfortably at prices within the range of an average family's salary.
- **Shelter:** Although accommodations vary in size and quality, every family has access to a comfortable home or apartment, heated and cooled, with gas or electricity for cooking, and electric lighting, all for a reasonable rate.

Only the three basic necessities of food, clothing, and shelter have been mentioned. The average American citizen has other privileges and advantages available in return for modest effort, not exceeding eight hours per day of labor. Among these is the privilege of automobile transportation, with which one can go and come at will, at very small cost.

The average American has security of property rights not found in any other country in the world. Surplus money can be placed in a bank with the assurance that the government will protect it and make good if the bank fails. U.S. citizens can travel from one state to another without a passport. Americans may go when they please and return at will. In most other countries, the people cannot travel with so much freedom and at so little cost.

> The three basic necessities—food, clothing, and shelter—can be obtained with a modicum of effort, freeing us to *think and grow rich*.

## Recognize the "miracle" that has provided these blessings

We often hear politicians proclaiming the freedom of America when they solicit votes, but seldom do they take the time or devote sufficient effort to analyze the source or nature of this "freedom." Having no axe to grind, no grudge, no ulterior motives, I have the privilege of going into a frank analysis of that mysterious, abstract, greatly misunderstood *"something"* which gives to every citizen of America more blessings, more opportunities to accumulate wealth, more freedom of every nature, than may be found in any other country.

I have the right to analyze the source and nature of this *unseen power*, because I know, and have known for more than a quarter of a century, many of the people who organized that power and many who have been responsible for its maintenance.

The name of this mysterious benefactor of mankind is *capital*!

*Capital* consists not only of money, but more particularly of highly organized, intelligent groups of people who plan ways and means of using money efficiently for the good of the public and to profit themselves.

These groups consist of scientists, educators, chemists, inventors, business analysts, public relations experts, transportation experts, accountants, lawyers, doctors, and others who have highly specialized knowledge in all fields of industry and business. They pioneer, experiment, and blaze trails in new fields of endeavor. They support colleges, hospitals, and public schools, build good roads, publish newspapers, pay most of the cost of government, and take care of the multitudinous details that drive human progress. Stated briefly, the capitalists are the brains of civilization, because they supply the entire fabric of which all education, enlightenment, and human progress consists.

Money, without brains, is always dangerous. Properly used, it is the most important essential of civilization. A simple breakfast for a New York family consisting of grapefruit juice, cereal, eggs, bread and butter, and coffee with sugar could not be provided at a reasonable price if organized capital had not provided the machinery, the ships, the railroads, and the trained people to operate them.

---

> Money, without brains, is always dangerous.
> Together, they fuel the progress of civilization.

---

Steam ships and railroads do not spring up from the earth and function automatically. They come in response to the call of civilization, through the labor and ingenuity and organizing ability of people who have *imagination, faith, enthusiasm, decision, and persistence!* These people are known as capitalists. They are motivated by the desire to build, construct, achieve, render useful service, earn profits and accumulate riches. And, because they *render service without which there would be no civilization*, they put themselves in the way of great riches.

Just to keep the record simple and understandable, I will add that these capitalists are the selfsame people of whom most of us have heard soapbox orators speak. They are the same people to whom radicals, racketeers, dishonest politicians, and grafting labor leaders refer as "the predatory interests," or "Wall Street."

I am not attempting to present an argument for or against any group of people or any system of economics. I am not attempting to condemn collective bargaining when I refer to "grafting labor leaders," nor do I aim to give a clean bill of health to all individuals known as capitalists.

The purpose of this book—a purpose to which I have faithfully devoted over a quarter of a century—is to present to all who want the knowledge, the most dependable philosophy through which individuals may accumulate riches in whatever amounts they desire.

I have here analyzed the economic advantages of the capitalistic system for the two-fold purpose of showing:

- That all who seek riches must recognize and adapt themselves to the system that controls all approaches to fortunes, large or small, and
- To present the side of the picture opposite to that being shown by politicians and demagogues who deliberately becloud the issues they bring up, by referring to organized capital as if it were something poisonous

This is a capitalistic country, it was developed through the use of capital, and we who claim the right to partake of the blessings of freedom and opportunity, we who seek to accumulate riches here, may as well know that neither riches nor opportunity would be available to us if *organized capital* had not provided these benefits.

If you are one of those who believe that riches can be accumulated by the mere act of people who organize themselves into groups and demand *more pay* for *less service*, if you are one of those who *demand* Government relief without early morning disturbance when the money is delivered to you, if you are one of those who believe in trading their votes to politicians in return for the passing of laws which permit the raiding of the public treasury, you may rest securely on your belief, with certain knowledge that no one will disturb you, because *this is a free country where every person may think as he pleases*, where nearly everybody can live with but little effort, where many may live well without doing any work whatsoever.

However, you should know the full truth concerning this *freedom* of which so many people boast and so few understand. As great as it is, as far as it reaches, as many privileges as it provides, *it does not and cannot bring riches without effort.*

## Honor the law of economics

There is but one dependable method of accumulating and legally holding riches and that is by selling a product or service. No system has ever been created by which people can legally acquire riches through mere force of numbers or without giving in return something of value.

There is a principle known as the *law of economics!* This is more than a theory. It is a law no person can break without suffering serious consequences.

---

According to the *law of economics*,
the only way to profit legally is to exchange
a product or service for more money
than it cost to provide that product or service.

---

Mark well the name of the principle and remember it, because it is far more powerful than all the politicians and political machines. It is above and beyond the control of all the labor unions. It cannot be swayed or influenced or bribed by racketeers or self-appointed leaders in any calling. Moreover, *it has an all-seeing eye and a perfect system of bookkeeping*, in which it keeps an accurate account of the transactions of every human being engaged in the business of trying to get without giving. Sooner or later its auditors come around, look over the records of individuals both great and small, and demand an accounting.

"Wall Street, Big Business, Capital Predatory Interests," or whatever name you choose to give the system which has given us *American freedom*, represents a group of people who understand, respect, and adapt themselves to this powerful *law of economics!* Their financial continuation depends upon their respecting the law.

The *law of economics* was passed by Nature! There is no Supreme Court to which violators of this law may appeal. The law hands out both penalties for its violation and appropriate rewards for its observance, without interference or the possibility of interference by any human being. The law cannot be repealed. It is as fixed as the stars in the heavens and subject to and a part of the same system that controls the stars.

May one refuse to adapt one's self to the *law of economics?*

Certainly! This is a free country, where all are born with equal rights, including the privilege of ignoring the *law of economics*.

What happens then?

Well, nothing happens until large numbers of people join forces for the avowed purpose of ignoring the law and taking what they want by force. *Then comes the dictator, with well-organized firing squads and machine guns!*

We have not yet reached that stage in America! But we have heard all we want to know about how the system works. Perhaps we shall be fortunate enough not to demand personal knowledge of so gruesome a reality. Doubtless we shall prefer to continue with our *freedom of speech, freedom of deed,* and *freedom to render useful service in return for riches.*

The practice, by government officials, of extending to men and women the privilege of raiding the public treasury in return for votes, sometimes results in election, but as night follows day, the final payoff comes: when every penny wrongfully used, must be repaid with compound interest on compound interest. If those who make the grab are not forced to repay, the burden falls on their children and their children's children, "even unto the third and fourth generations." There is no way to avoid the debt.

People can, and sometimes do, form themselves into groups for the purpose of crowding wages up and working hours down. There is a point beyond which they cannot go. It is the point at which the *law of economics* steps in, shuttering the business and letting all employees go.

These observations are not founded upon short-time experience. They are the result of twenty-five years of careful analysis of the methods of both the most successful and the most unsuccessful people America has known.

## Look for and seize opportunity

*Opportunity* has spread its wares before you. Step up to the front, select what you want, create your plan, put the plan into action, and follow through with *persistence*. "Capitalistic" America will do the rest. You can depend upon this much—*Capitalistic America ensures every person the opportunity to render useful service and collect riches in proportion to the value of the service.*

The "System" denies no one this right, but it does not and cannot promise *something for nothing*, because the *law of economics*, itself, irrevocably controls the system that neither recognizes nor tolerates for long *getting without giving*.

> *Capitalistic America ensures every person the opportunity to render useful service and collect riches in proportion to the value of the service.*

America provides all the freedom and all the opportunity to accumulate riches that any honest person may require. When one goes hunting for game, one selects hunting grounds where game is plentiful. When seeking riches, the same rule naturally applies. Think twice, you who are seeking riches, before trying to destroy the Capitalistic System of a country whose citizens spend hundreds of million dollars a year for luxury items that people in most nations can only dream about.

Remember, also, that the business of producing, transporting, and marketing these items of merchandise gives regular employment to *many millions of men and women*, who receive for their services *many millions of dollars monthly*, and spend it freely for both luxuries and necessities. Behind all this exchange of merchandise and personal services may be found an abundance of *opportunity* to accumulate riches.

Here our *American freedom* comes to one's aid. There is nothing to stop you or anyone from engaging in any portion of the effort necessary to carry on these businesses. If one has superior talent, training, and experience, one may accumulate riches in large amounts. Those not so fortunate may accumulate smaller amounts. Anyone may earn a living in return for a very nominal amount of labor.

You are the master of your own earthly destiny just as surely as you have the power to control your own thoughts.

Take inventory of yourself and find out how many of the "ghosts" are standing in your way.

Liberate yourself from the six ghosts of fear.

# Step 3

# Outwit the Six Ghosts of Fear

*Before you* can put any portion of this philosophy into successful use, your mind must be prepared to receive it. The preparation is not difficult. It begins with study, analysis, and understanding of three enemies that you must clear out: *indecision, doubt,* and *fear!*

The sixth sense will never function while any of these three negatives remain in your mind. The members of this unholy trio are closely related; where one is found, the other two are close at hand.

*Indecision* is the seedling of *fear!* Remember this, as you read. Indecision crystallizes into *doubt,* the two blend and become *fear!* The "blending" process often is slow. This is one reason why these three enemies are so dangerous. They germinate and grow without their presence being observed.

The remainder of this chapter describes an end that must be attained before the philosophy, as a whole, can be put into practical use. It also analyzes a condition that has reduced huge numbers of people to poverty, and it states a truth that must be understood by all who accumulate riches, whether measured in terms of money or a state of mind of far greater value than money.

The purpose of this chapter is to turn the spotlight of attention upon the cause and the cure of the six basic fears. Before we can master an enemy, we must know its name, its habits, and its place of abode. As you read, analyze yourself carefully, and determine which, if any, of the six common fears have attached themselves to you.

Do not be deceived by the habits of these subtle enemies. Sometimes they remain hidden in the subconscious mind, where they are difficult to locate and still more difficult to eliminate.

## The six basic fears

There are six basic fears, with some combination of which every human suffers at one time or another. Most people are fortunate if they do not suffer from the entire six. Named in the order of their most common appearance, they are:

- Fear of *poverty*
- Fear of *criticism*
- Fear of *ill health*
- Fear of *lost love*
- Fear of *old age*
- Fear of *death*

All other fears are of minor importance and can be grouped under these six headings.

The prevalence of these fears, as a curse to the world, runs in cycles. For almost six years, during the Great Depression, we floundered in the cycle of *fear of poverty*. During the periods when we were at war or faced with terror, we were in the cycle of *fear of death*. Even in periods of prosperity and peace, we are in the cycle of *fear of ill health*, as evidenced by the epidemic of various diseases which spread themselves all over the world.

*Fears are nothing more than states of mind.* One's state of mind is subject to control and direction. Physicians, as everyone knows, are less subject to attack by disease than ordinary laypersons, for the reason that physicians *do not fear disease*. Physicians, without fear or hesitation, have been known to physically contact hundreds of people daily suffering from such contagious diseases as smallpox, without becoming infected. Their immunity against the disease consisted, largely, if not solely, in their absolute lack of *fear*.

We can create nothing that is not first conceived in the form of an impulse of thought. Following this statement, comes another of still greater importance; namely, *thought impulses begin immediately to translate themselves into their physical equivalent, whether those thoughts are voluntary or involuntary.* Thought impulses that are picked up through the ether, by mere chance (thoughts which have been released by other minds) may determine one's financial, business, professional, or social destiny just as surely as do the thought impulses which one creates by intent and design.

---

Thought impulses begin immediately to translate themselves into their physical equivalent, whether those thoughts are voluntary or involuntary.

---

We are here laying the foundation for the presentation of a fact of great importance to the person who does not understand why some people appear to be "lucky" while others of equal or greater ability, training, experience, and brain capacity, seem destined to ride with misfortune. This fact may be explained by the statement that human beings have the ability to completely control their own minds, and with this control, obviously, may open their minds to the tramp thought impulses which are being released by other brains, or close the doors tightly and admit only thought impulses of their own choice.

Nature has endowed us with absolute control over but one thing, and that is *thought*. This fact, coupled with the additional fact that everything people create begins in the form of a thought, leads one very near to the principle by which *fear* may be mastered.

If it is true that *all thought has a tendency to clothe itself in its physical equivalent* (and this is true beyond any reasonable room for doubt), it is equally true that thought impulses of fear and poverty cannot be translated into courage and financial gain.

After the Wall Street crash of 1929, people in the U.S. and other industrialized countries were compelled to think of poverty. Slowly, but surely that mass thought was crystallized into its physical equivalent, which was known as a "depression." This had to happen in conformity with the laws of Nature.

## Fear of poverty

There can be no compromise between *poverty* and *riches!* The two roads that lead to poverty and riches travel in opposite directions. If you want riches, you must refuse to accept any circumstance that leads toward poverty. (The word "riches" is here used in its broadest sense, meaning financial, spiritual, mental, and material estates.) The starting point of the path that leads to riches is *desire*, which is covered in Step 5, but you must first prepare your mind to make practical use of *desire*.

Here, then, is the place to give yourself a challenge that will definitely determine how much of this philosophy you have absorbed. Here is the point at which you can turn prophet and foretell, accurately, what the future holds in store for you. If, after reading this chapter, you are willing to accept poverty, you may as well make up your mind to receive poverty. This is one decision you cannot avoid.

If you demand riches, determine what form and how much will be required to satisfy you. You know the road that leads to riches. You have been given a road map, which, if followed, will keep you on that road. If you neglect to make the start, or you stop before you arrive, no one will be to blame but *you*. This responsibility is yours. No excuse will save you from accepting the responsibility if you now fail or refuse to demand riches of Life, because the acceptance calls for but one thing—incidentally, the only thing you can control—and that is a *state of mind*. A state of mind is something that one assumes. It cannot be purchased; it must be created.

Fear of poverty is a state of mind, nothing else! But it is sufficient to destroy one's chances of achievement in any undertaking. This fear paralyzes the faculty of reason, destroys the faculty of imagination, kills off self-reliance, undermines enthusiasm, discourages initiative, leads to uncertainty of purpose, encourages procrastination, wipes out enthusiasm and makes self-control impossible. It takes the charm from one's personality, destroys the possibility of accurate thinking, diverts concentration of effort, masters persistence, turns willpower into nothingness, destroys ambition, beclouds the memory, and invites failure in every conceivable form; it kills love and assassinates the finer emotions of the heart, discourages friendship and invites disaster in a hundred forms, leads to sleeplessness, misery and unhappiness—and all this despite the obvious truth that we live in a world of overabundance of everything the heart could desire, with nothing standing between us and our desires, excepting lack of a definite purpose.

*Fear of poverty* is, without doubt, the most destructive of the six basic fears. It has been placed at the head of the list, because it is the most difficult to master. Considerable courage is required to state the truth about the origin of this fear, and still greater courage to accept the truth after it has been stated. The fear of poverty grew out of the human tendency to *prey upon others economically.* Nearly all animals lower than humans are motivated by instinct and their capacity to think is limited; therefore, they prey upon one another physically. Humans, with their superior sense of intuition, with the capacity to think and to reason, do not eat other humans bodily; they get more satisfaction out of "eating" them *financially.*

Of all the ages of the world of which we know anything, the age in which we live seems to be one that is outstanding because of money madness. People are considered less than the dust of the earth unless they can display a fat bank account, but if they have money—*never mind how acquired*—they are too often idolized and treated as being above the law. They rule in politics, dominate in business, and the whole world about them bow in respect when they pass by.

Nothing brings so much suffering and humility as *poverty!* Only those who have experienced poverty understand the full meaning of this.

It is no wonder that we fear poverty. Through a long line of inherited experiences we have learned, for sure, that some people cannot be trusted where matters of money and earthly possessions are concerned. This is a rather stinging indictment, the worst part of it being that it is *true.*

Many marriages are motivated by the wealth possessed by one or both of the contracting parties. It is no wonder, therefore, that the divorce courts are busy.

So eager are people to possess wealth that they will acquire it in any feasible manner—through legal methods if possible—through other methods if necessary or expedient.

Self-analysis may disclose weaknesses that one does not like to acknowledge. This form of examination is essential to all who demand of Life more than mediocrity and poverty. Remember, as you check yourself point by point, that you are the court and the jury, the prosecuting attorney and the defense attorney, the plaintiff and the defendant, and that you are on trial. Face the facts squarely. Ask yourself definite questions and demand direct replies. When the examination is over, you will know more about yourself. If you do not feel that you can be an impartial judge in this self-examination, call upon someone who knows you well to serve as judge while you cross-examine yourself. You are after the truth. Get it, no matter at what cost even though it may temporarily embarrass you!

The majority of people, if asked what they fear most, would reply, "I fear nothing." The reply would be inaccurate, because few people realize that they are bound, handicapped, whipped spiritually and physically through some form of fear. So subtle and deeply seated is the emotion of fear that one may go through life burdened with it, never recognizing its presence. Only a courageous analysis will disclose the presence of this universal enemy. When you begin such an analysis, search deeply into your character. Here is a list of the symptoms for which you should look:

## Symptoms of the fear of poverty

**Indifference:** Commonly expressed through lack of ambition; willingness to tolerate poverty; acceptance of whatever compensation life may offer without protest; mental and physical laziness; and lack of initiative, imagination, enthusiasm, and self-control.

**Indecision:** The habit of permitting others to do one's thinking. Staying "on the fence."

**Doubt:** Generally expressed through excuses designed to cover up, explain away, or apologize for one's failures, sometimes expressed in the form of envy or criticism of those who are successful.

**Worry:** Usually expressed by finding fault with others, a tendency to spend beyond one's income, neglect of personal appearance, scowling, and frowning; intemperance in the use of alcoholic drink or the use of narcotics; nervousness, lack of poise, self-consciousness, and lack of self-reliance.

**Over-caution:** The habit of looking for the negative side of every circumstance—thinking and talking of possible failure instead of concentrating upon the means of succeeding. Knowing all the roads to disaster, but never searching for the plans to avoid failure. Waiting for "the right time" to begin putting ideas and plans into action, until the waiting becomes a permanent habit. Remembering those who have failed and forgetting those who have succeeded. Seeing the hole in the doughnut, but overlooking the doughnut.

**Procrastination:** The habit of putting off until tomorrow matters that should have been done last year; spending enough time in creating excuses to have done the job (this symptom is closely related to over-caution, doubt, and worry); refusal to accept responsibility when it can be avoided; willingness to compromise rather than put up a stiff fight; compromising with difficulties instead of harnessing and using them as stepping stones to advancement; bargaining with life for a penny, instead of demanding prosperity, opulence, riches, contentment, and happiness; and planning what to do *if and when overtaken by failure, instead of burning all bridges and making retreat impossible.* This is manifested further by weakness of, and often total lack of self-confidence, definiteness of purpose, self-control, initiative, enthusiasm, ambition, thrift, and sound reasoning ability, *expecting poverty instead of demanding riches,* and association with those who accept poverty instead of seeking the company of those who demand and receive riches.

## Fear of criticism

Most people are at the least very uncomfortable when criticized and in some cases may become depressed and despondent when others censure them. The fear of criticism robs people of their initiative, destroys their power of imagination, limits their individuality, takes away their self-reliance, and does them damage in a hundred other ways. Parents often cause their children irreparable injury by criticizing them. The mother of one of my boyhood chums used to punish him with a switch almost daily, always completing the job with the statement, "You'll land in the penitentiary before you are twenty." He was sent to a Reformatory at the age of seventeen.

Criticism is the one form of service of which everyone has too much. Everyone has a stock of it that is handed out, gratis, whether called for or not. One's nearest relatives often are the worst offenders. It should be recognized as a crime (in reality it is a crime of the worst nature), for any parent to build inferiority complexes in the mind of a child, through unnecessary criticism. Employers, who understand human nature, get the best there is in people, not by criticism, but by constructive suggestion. Parents may accomplish the same results with their children. Criticism will plant *fear* or resentment in the human heart, but it will not build love or affection.

## Fear of ill health

This fear may be traced to both physical and social heredity. It is closely associated, as to its origin, with the causes of fear of old age and the fear of death, because it leads one closely to the border of "terrible worlds" of which nothing is really known, but concerning which some discomforting stories have been told. The opinion is somewhat general, also, that certain unethical people engaged in the business of selling health have had not a little to do with keeping alive the fear of ill health.

In the main, ill health is feared because of the suffering it causes and fear and uncertainty of what may happen when death comes. In addition there is the fear of the economic toll it may claim.

A reputable physician estimated that 75% of all people who visit physicians for professional service are suffering with hypochondria (imaginary illness). It has been shown most convincingly that the fear of disease, even where there is not the slightest cause for fear, often produces the physical symptoms of the disease feared. Powerful and mighty is the human mind! It can cure or inflict illness.

Through a series of experiments conducted some years ago, it was proved that people might be made ill by suggestion. We conducted this experiment by causing three acquaintances to visit the "victims," each of whom asked the question, "What ails you? You look terribly ill." The first questioner usually provoked a grin and a nonchalant "Oh, nothing, I'm all right," from the victim. The second questioner usually was answered with the statement, "I don't know exactly, but I do feel badly." The third questioner was usually met with the frank admission that the victim was actually feeling ill.

Try this on an acquaintance if you doubt that it will make him uncomfortable, but do not carry the experiment too far.

In some primitive cultures, people take vengeance upon their enemies by placing a spell on the victim. Because they believe the spell is real, they do become sick and often die.

There is overwhelming evidence that disease sometimes begins in the form of negative thought impulse. Such an impulse may be passed from one mind to another, by suggestion, or created by an individual in his or her own mind.

Doctors sometimes send patients into new climates for their health, because a change of "mental attitude" is necessary. The seed of fear of ill health lives in every human mind. Worry, fear, discouragement, disappointment in love and business affairs cause this seed to germinate and grow.

## Fear of lost love

The original source of this inherent fear needs but little description, because it obviously grew out of ancient man's polygamous habit of stealing his fellowman's mate, and his habit of taking liberties with her whenever he could.

The fear of lost love is the most painful of all the six basic fears. It probably plays more havoc with the body and mind than any of the other basic fears.

One of the distinguishing symptoms of this fear is *jealousy*: the habit of being suspicious of friends and loved ones without any reasonable evidence of sufficient grounds. Another is the habit of accusing wife or husband of infidelity without grounds. Another symptom is a general suspicion of everyone, absolute faith in no one, and the habit of finding fault with friends, relatives, business associates, and loved ones upon the slightest provocation, or without any cause whatsoever.

## Fear of old age

The possibility of ill health, which is more common as people grow older, is a major cause of this common fear of old age. Eroticism also enters into the cause of the fear of old age, as no man cherishes the thought of diminishing sex attraction.

Another contributing cause of the fear of old age is the possibility of loss of freedom and independence, as old age may bring with it the loss of both physical and economic freedom.

Some people show a tendency to slow down and develop an inferiority complex when they get older, falsely believing one's self to be "slipping" because of age. (The truth is that some of our most useful years, mentally and spiritually, are those in later years. Unfortunately there are older men and women who lose their initiative, imagination, and self-reliance by falsely believing themselves too old to exercise these qualities

## Fear of death

To some this is the cruelest of all the basic fears. The reason is obvious. We know not what to expect after death. As Shakespeare stated so well in *Hamlet*, death is "the undiscovered country from whose bourne no traveler returns."

The fear of *death* is not as common now as it was during the age when there were no great colleges and universities. Men of science have turned the spotlight of truth upon the world, and this truth is rapidly freeing men and women from this terrible fear of *death*. Through the aid of biology, astronomy, geology, and other related sciences, the fears of the dark ages that gripped the minds of men and destroyed their reason have been dispelled.

This fear is useless. Death will come no matter what anyone may think about it. Accept it as a necessity and pass the thought out of your mind. It must be a necessity, or it would not come to all.

Keep in mind that the entire world is made up of only two things, *energy* and *matter*. In elementary physics we learn that neither matter nor energy (the only two realities known to man) can be created or destroyed. Both matter and energy can be transformed, but neither can be destroyed.

Life is energy, if it is anything. If neither energy nor matter can be destroyed, life cannot be destroyed. Life, like other forms of energy, may be passed through various processes of transition, or change, but it cannot be destroyed. Death is mere transition.

If death is not mere change or transition, then nothing comes after death except a long, eternal peaceful sleep, and sleep is nothing to be feared. Thus you may wipe out, forever, the fear of death.

## Worry

Worry is a state of mind based upon fear. It works slowly, but persistently. It is insidious and subtle. Step by step it digs itself in until it paralyzes one's reasoning faculty, destroying self-confidence and initiative. Worry is a form of sustained fear caused by indecision; therefore, it is a state of mind that can be controlled.

An unsettled mind is helpless. Indecision makes an unsettled mind. Most individuals lack the willpower to reach decisions promptly and to stand by them after they have been made, even during normal business conditions. During periods of economic unrest people are handicapped, not alone by their inherent nature to be slow at reaching decisions, but they are influenced by the indecision of others around them who have created a state of "mass indecision." The six basic fears become translated into a state of worry, through indecision.

## Become fearless

You can overcome all fears:

- Relieve yourself forever of the *fear of death*, by reaching a decision to accept death as an inescapable event.
- Whip the *fear of poverty* by reaching a decision to get along with whatever wealth you can accumulate *without worry*.
- Put your foot upon the neck of the *fear of criticism* by reaching a decision *not to worry* about what other people think, do, or say.
- Eliminate the *fear of old age* by reaching a decision to accept it, not as a handicap, but as a great blessing that carries with it wisdom, self-control, and understanding not known to youth.
- Acquit yourself of the *fear of ill health* by the decision to forget symptoms.
- Master the *fear of lost love* by reaching a decision to get along without love, if necessary.
- Kill the *habit of worry*, in all its forms, by reaching a general, blanket decision that nothing life has to offer is worth the price of worry. With this decision will come poise, peace of mind, and calmness of thought that will bring happiness.

## An obligation to yourself and everyone else

A person whose mind is filled with fear not only destroys his or her own chances of intelligent action, but also transmits these destructive vibrations to the minds of other people, destroying their chances.

Even a dog or a horse knows when its master lacks courage; moreover, a dog or a horse will pick up the vibrations of fear thrown off by its master and behave accordingly. Lower down the line of intelligence in the animal kingdom, one finds this same capacity to pick up the vibrations of fear. A honeybee immediately senses fear in the mind of a person. For reasons unknown, a bee will sting the person whose mind is releasing vibrations of fear much more readily than it will molest the person whose mind registers no fear.

The vibrations of fear pass from one mind to another just as quickly and as surely as the sound of the human voice passes from the broadcasting station to the receiving station and by *the self-same medium*.

Mental telepathy is a reality. Thoughts pass from one mind to another, voluntarily, whether or not this fact is recognized by either the person releasing the thoughts or the persons who pick up those thoughts.

---

> A person whose mind is filled with fear not only destroys his or her own chances of intelligent action, but also transmits these destructive vibrations to the minds of other people, destroying their chances.

---

The person who gives expression, by word of mouth, to negative or destructive thoughts is practically certain to experience the results of those words in the form of a destructive "kickback." The release of destructive thought impulses, alone, without the aid of words, produces also a "kickback" in more ways than one:

- First of all, and perhaps most important to be remembered, the person who releases thoughts of a destructive nature must suffer damage through the breaking down of the faculty of creative imagination.
- Secondly, the presence in the mind of any destructive emotion develops a negative personality that repels people and often converts them into antagonists.
- The third source of damage to the person who entertains or releases negative thoughts, lies in this significant fact: these thought-impulses are not only damaging to others, but they *imbed themselves in the subconscious mind of the persons releasing them* and there become a part of their characters.

One is never through with a thought, merely by releasing it. When a thought is released, it spreads in every direction, through the medium of the ether, but it also plants itself permanently in the subconscious mind of the person releasing it.

Presumably, your business in life is to achieve success. To be successful, you must find peace of mind, acquire the material needs of life, and above all, attain *happiness*. All of these evidences of success begin in the form of thought impulses.

You may control your own mind; you have the power to feed it whatever thought impulses you choose. With this privilege goes also the responsibility of using it constructively. You are the master of your own earthly destiny just as surely as you have the power to control your own thoughts. You may influence, direct, and eventually control your own environment, making your life what you want it to be. On the other hand, you may neglect to exercise the privilege that is yours—to make your life to order, thus casting yourself upon the broad sea of "Circumstance" where you will be tossed hither and yon, like a chip on the waves of the ocean.

The most common weakness of all human beings is the habit of leaving their minds open to the negative influence of other people.

You have *absolute control* over but one thing: your thoughts.

The mind can produce anything the mind can conceive and believe.

# Step 4

# Eliminate Negative Thinking: The Seventh Basic Evil

In addition to the *six basic fears*, there is another evil by which people suffer. It constitutes a rich soil in which the seeds of failure grow abundantly. It is so subtle that its presence often is undetected. This affliction cannot properly be classed as a fear. *It is more deeply seated and more often fatal than all of the six fears* described in the previous chapter. For want of a better name, let us call this evil *susceptibility to negative influences*.

People who accumulate great riches always protect themselves against this evil! The poverty stricken never do! Those who succeed in any calling must prepare their minds to resist the evil. If you are reading this philosophy for the purpose of accumulating riches, you should examine yourself very carefully to determine whether you are susceptible to negative influences. If you neglect this self-analysis, you will forfeit your right to attain the object of your desires.

Make the analysis searching. After you read the questions prepared for this self-analysis, hold yourself to a strict accounting in your answers. Go at the task as carefully as you would search for any other enemy you knew to be awaiting you in ambush and deal with your own faults as you would with a more tangible enemy.

---

The seventh basic evil is *susceptibility to negative influences*. It is more deeply seated and more often fatal than all of the six fears.

---

You can easily protect yourself against highway robbers, because the law provides organized cooperation for your benefit, but this *seventh basic evil* is more difficult to overcome, because it strikes when you are unaware of its presence, when you are asleep, and while you are awake. Moreover, its weapon is intangible, because it consists merely of a *state of mind*. This evil is also dangerous because it strikes in as many different forms as there are human experiences. Sometimes it enters the mind through the well-intentioned words of one's own relatives. At other times, it bores from within, through one's own mental attitude. Always it is as deadly as poison, even though it may not kill as quickly.

## How to protect yourself against negative influences

To protect yourself against negative influences, whether of your own making or the result of the activities of negative people around you, take the following steps:

1. Recognize that you have *willpower* and put it into constant use, until it builds a wall of immunity against negative influences in your own mind. Recognize the fact that you, and every other human being, are, by nature, lazy, indifferent, and susceptible to all suggestions that harmonize with your weaknesses.
2. Recognize that you are, by nature, susceptible to all the six basic fears and set up habits for the purpose of counteracting them.
3. Recognize that negative influences often work on you through your subconscious mind; therefore, they are difficult to detect.
4. Keep your mind closed against all people who depress or discourage you in any way.
5. Deliberately seek the company of people who influence you to think and act for yourself.
6. Do not *expect* troubles, because such expectations have a tendency to be fulfilled.

*Without doubt, the most common weakness of all human beings is the habit of leaving their minds open to the negative influence of other people.* This weakness is all the more damaging, because most people do not recognize that they are cursed by it, and many who acknowledge it neglect or refuse to correct the evil until it becomes an uncontrollable part of their daily habits.

---

The most common weakness
of all human beings is the habit of
leaving their minds open to the
negative influence of other people.

---

The following list of questions can help you see yourself as you really are. Read the questions and state your answers aloud, so you can hear your own voice. This will make it easier for you to be truthful with yourself.

## Self-Analysis Test Questions

- Do you complain often of "feeling bad," and if so, what is the cause?
- Do you find fault with other people at the slightest provocation?
- Do you frequently make mistakes in your work, and if so, why?
- Are you sarcastic and offensive in your conversation?
- Do you deliberately avoid the association of anyone, and if so, why?
- Do you suffer frequently with indigestion? If so, what is the cause?
- Does life seem futile and the future hopeless to you? If so, why?
- Do you like your occupation? If not, why not?

- Do you often feel self-pity, and if so why?
- Are you envious of those who excel you?
- To which do you devote most time, thinking of success or of failure?
- Are you gaining or losing self-confidence as you grow older?
- Do you learn something of value from all mistakes?
- Are you permitting some relative or acquaintance to worry you? If so, why?
- Are you sometimes "in the clouds" and at other times in the depths of despondency?
- Who has the most inspiring influence upon you? For what reason?
- Do you tolerate negative or discouraging influences that you can avoid?
- Are you careless in your personal appearance? If so, when and why?
- Have you learned how to "drown your troubles" by being too busy to be annoyed by them?
- Would you call yourself a "spineless weakling" if you permitted others to do your thinking for you?
- Do you neglect internal bathing until autointoxication makes you ill-tempered and irritable?
- How many preventable disturbances annoy you, and why do you tolerate them?
- Do you resort to liquor, narcotics, or cigarettes to "quiet your nerves"? If so, why do you not try willpower instead?
- Does anyone "nag" you, and if so, for what reason?

- Do you have a *definite major purpose*, and if so, what is it, and what plan have you for achieving it?
- Do you suffer from any of the *six basic fears?* If so, which ones?
- Have you a method by which you can shield yourself against the negative influence of others?
- Do you make deliberate use of autosuggestion to nurture a positive mindset?
- Which do you value most, your material possessions or your privilege of controlling your own thoughts?
- Do others easily influence you against your own judgment?
- Has today added anything of value to your stock of knowledge or state of mind?
- Do you face squarely the circumstances that make you unhappy, or do you sidestep the responsibility?
- Do you analyze all mistakes and failures and try to profit by them, or do you take the attitude that this is not your duty?
- Can you name three of your most damaging weaknesses? What are you doing to correct them?
- Do you encourage other people to bring their worries to you for sympathy?
- Do you choose, from your daily experiences, lessons or influences that aid in your personal advancement?
- Does your presence have a negative influence on other people as a rule?
- What habits of other people annoy you most?
- Do you form your own opinions or permit yourself to be influenced by other people?

- Have you learned how to create a mental state of mind with which you can shield yourself against all discouraging influences?
- Does your occupation inspire you with faith and hope?
- Are you conscious of possessing spiritual forces of sufficient power to enable you to keep your mind free from all forms of *fear*?
- Does your religion help you to keep your own mind positive?
- Do you feel it your duty to share other people's worries? If so, why?
- If you believe that "birds of a feather flock together"? What have you learned about yourself by studying the friends whom you attract?
- What connection, if any, do you see between the people with whom you associate most closely and any unhappiness you may experience?
- Could it be possible that some person whom you consider to be a friend is, in reality, your worst enemy because of his or her negative influence on your mind?
- By what rules do you judge who is helpful and who is damaging to you?
- Are your intimate associates mentally superior or inferior to you?
- How much time out of every 24 hours do you devote to:
    - your occupation
    - sleep
    - play and relaxation
    - acquiring useful knowledge
    - plain waste?

- Who among your acquaintances
  - encourages you most
  - cautions you most
  - discourages you most
  - helps you most in other ways?
- What is your greatest worry? Why do you tolerate it?
- When others offer you free, unsolicited advice, do you accept it without question, or analyze their motive?
- What, above all else, do you most *desire*? Do you intend to acquire it? Are you willing to subordinate all other desires for this one? How much time daily do you devote to acquiring it?
- Do you change your mind often? If so, why?
- Do you usually finish everything you begin?
- Are you easily impressed by other people's business or professional titles, college degrees, or wealth?
- Are you easily influenced by what other people think or say of you?
- Do you cater to people because of their social or financial status?
- Whom do you believe to be the greatest person living? In what respect is this person superior to you?
- How much time have you devoted to studying and answering these questions? (At least one day is necessary for the analysis and the answering of the entire list.)

If you have answered all these questions truthfully, you know more about yourself than the majority of people know about themselves. Study the questions carefully. Come back to them once each week for several months, and be astounded at the amount of additional knowledge, of great value to yourself, you will have gained by the simple method of answering the questions truthfully. If you are uncertain concerning the answers to some of the questions, seek the counsel of those who know you well, especially those who have no motive to flatter you, and see yourself through their eyes. The experience will be astonishing.

You have *absolute control* over but one thing, and that is your thoughts. This is the most significant and inspiring of all known facts! It reflects our divine nature. This divine prerogative is the sole means by which you may control your own destiny. If you fail to control your own mind, you may be sure you will control nothing else.

---

You have *absolute control* over but one thing: your thoughts.

---

If you must be careless with your possessions, let it be in connection with material things. Your mind is your spiritual estate! Protect and use it with the care to which Divine Royalty is entitled. You were given *willpower* for this purpose.

Unfortunately, there is no legal protection against those who, either by design or ignorance, poison the minds of others by negative thought or suggestion. This form of destruction should be punishable by heavy legal penalties, because it may and often does destroy one's chances of acquiring material things that are protected by law.

People with negative minds tried to convince Thomas A. Edison that he could not build a machine that would record and reproduce the human voice, "because" they said, "no one else had ever produced such a machine." Edison did not believe them. He knew that the mind could produce *anything the mind could conceive and believe,* and that knowledge was the thing that lifted the great Edison above the common herd.

---

> Thomas Edison knew that the mind could produce anything the mind could conceive and believe.

---

Men with negative minds told F. W. Woolworth, he would go broke trying to run a store on five and ten cent sales. He did not believe them. He knew that he could do anything, within reason, if he backed his plans with faith. Exercising his right to keep other men's negative suggestions out of his mind, he piled up a fortune of more than a hundred million dollars.

Men with negative minds told George Washington he could not hope to win against the vastly superior forces of the British, but he exercised his divine right to *believe*; hence, this book was published under the protection of the Stars and Stripes, while the name of Lord Cornwallis has been all but forgotten.

Doubting Thomases scoffed scornfully when Henry Ford tried out his first crudely built automobile on the streets of Detroit. Some said the thing never would become practical. Others said no one would pay money for such a contraption. *Ford said, "I'll belt the earth with dependable motor cars," and he did!* His decision to trust his own judgment piled up a fortune far greater than the next five generations of his descendants can squander. Henry Ford has been repeatedly mentioned, because he is an astounding example of what one with a mind of one's own, and a will to control it, can accomplish. His record knocks the foundation from under that timeworn excuse, "I never had a chance." Ford never had a chance, either, but he *created an opportunity and backed it with persistence until it made him richer than Croesus.*

---

> Ford never had a chance, but he *created an opportunity and backed it with persistence* until it made him richer than Croesus.

---

Mind control is the result of self-discipline and habit. You either control your mind or it controls you. There is no halfway compromise. The most practical of all methods for controlling the mind is the habit of keeping it busy with a definite purpose backed by a definite plan. Study the record of people who have achieved noteworthy success, and you will observe that they have control over their own minds, moreover, that they exercise that control and direct it toward the attainment of definite objectives. Without this control, success is not possible.

## Fifty-five famous excuses

People who do not succeed have one distinguishing trait in common: they have what they believe to be airtight excuses for their lack of achievement.

Some of these excuses are clever, and a few of them are justifiable by the facts. But excuses cannot be used for money. The world wants to know only one thing: *have you achieved success?*

---

> What you have accomplished is the only measure of your success.

---

A character analyst compiled a list of the most commonly used excuses. As you read the list, examine yourself carefully, and determine how many of these excuses, if any, are your own property. Remember, too, that the philosophy presented in this book makes every one of these excuses obsolete:

*If only* I didn't have a wife and family . . .
*If only* had enough "pull" . . .
*If only* I had money . . .
*If only* had a good education . . .
*If only* I could get a job . . .
*If only* I had good health . . .
*If only* I had more time . . .
*If only* times were better . . .
*If only* other people understood me . . .
*If only* conditions around me were different . . .
*If only* I could live my life over again . . .
*If only* I did not fear what *they* would say . . .
*If only* I had been given a chance . . .
*If only* I now had a chance . . .
*If only* other people didn't "have it in for me" . . .
*If only* nothing happens to stop me . . .
*If only* I were younger . . .
*If only* I could do what I want . . .
*If only* I had been born rich . . .
*If only* I could meet "the right people" . . .
*If only* I had the talent that some people have . . .
*If only* I dared assert myself . . .
*If only* I only had embraced past opportunities . . .
*If only* people didn't get on my nerves . . .

*If only* I didn't have to keep house and look after the children . . .
*If only* I could save some money . . .
*If only* the boss appreciated me . . .
*If only* I had somebody to help me . . .
*If only* my family understood me . . .
*If only* I lived in a big city . . .
*If only* I could just get started . . .
*If only* I were free . . .
*If only* I had the personality of some people . . .
*If only* I were not so fat . . .
*If only* my talents were known . . .
*If only* I could just get a "break" . . .
*If only* I could get out of debt . . .
*If only* I hadn't failed . . .
*If only* I knew how to . . .
*If only* everybody didn't oppose me . . .
*If only* I didn't have so many worries . . .
*If only* I could marry the right person . . .
*If only* people weren't so dumb . . .
*If only* my family were not so extravagant . . .
*If only* I were sure of myself . . .
*If only* luck were not against me . . .
*If only* I had not been born under the wrong star . . .
*If only* it were not true that "what is to be will be" . . .
*If only* I did not have to work so hard . . .
*If only* I hadn't lost my money . . .
*If only* I lived in a different neighborhood . . .
*If only* I didn't have a "past" . . .
*If only* I had a business of my own . . .
*If only* other people would listen to me . . .

*If only* . . . and this is the greatest of them all . . . I had the courage to see myself as I really am, I would find out what is wrong with me, and correct it, then I might have a chance to profit by my mistakes and learn something from the experience of others, because I know that there is something *wrong* with me, or I would now be where I *would have been if* I had spent more time analyzing my weaknesses and less time building excuses to cover them.

Building excuses to explain away failure is a national pastime. The habit is as old as the human race and is fatal to success! Why do people cling to their pet excuses? The answer is obvious: they defend their excuses because *they create* them!

An excuse is the child of one's own imagination. It is human nature to defend one's own brainchild.

Building excuses is a deeply rooted habit. Habits are difficult to break, especially when they provide justification for something we do. Plato had this truth in mind when he said, "The first and best victory is to conquer self. To be conquered by self is, of all things, the most shameful and vile."

---

### Excuses are no substitute for success.

---

Another philosopher had the same thought in mind when he said, "It was a great surprise to me when I discovered that most of the ugliness I saw in others was but a reflection of my own nature."

"It has always been a mystery to me," said Elbert Hubbard, "why people spend so much time deliberately fooling themselves by creating excuses to cover their weaknesses. If used differently, this same time would be sufficient to cure the weakness, then no excuses would be needed."

In parting, I would remind you that "life is a checkerboard, and the player opposite you is *time*. If you hesitate before moving, or neglect to move promptly, your checkers will be wiped off the board by *time*. You are playing against a partner who will not tolerate *indecision!*"

Previously you may have had a logical excuse for not having forced Life to come through with whatever you asked, but that excuse is now obsolete, because you are in possession of the Master Key that unlocks the door to Life's bountiful riches.

The Master Key is intangible, but it is powerful! It is the privilege of creating, in your own mind, a *burning desire* for a definite form of riches. There is no penalty for the use of the Key, but there is a price you must pay if you do not use it. The price is *failure*. There is a reward of stupendous proportions if you put the Key to use. It is the satisfaction that comes to all who conquer self and force Life to pay whatever is asked.

The reward is worthy of your effort. Will you make the start and be convinced?

"If we are related," said the immortal Emerson, "we shall meet." In closing, may I borrow his thought, and say, "If we are related, we have, through these pages, met."

Every noteworthy achievement begins with a *burning desire* for what one wants.

*Desire* backed by *faith* knows no such word as "impossible."

Only those who become *money conscious* ever accumulate great riches.

No more effort is required to demand abundance and prosperity than is required to accept misery and poverty.

# Step 5

# Develop a Burning Desire

Every noteworthy achievement begins with a *burning desire* for what one wants. If you do not first see great riches in your imagination, you will never see them in your bank balance. And never in the history of America has there been greater opportunity. We who are in this pursuit of riches should be encouraged to know that this dynamic world in which we live is demanding new ideas, new ways of doing things, new leaders, new inventions, new methods of teaching, new methods of marketing, new books, new literature, new applications for computers, new cures for diseases, and new approaches to every aspect of business and life. Opportunities are boundless.

Behind all this demand for new and better things, there is one quality one must possess to win: *a definite purpose*, the knowledge of what one wants and a burning *desire* to possess it.

> You must know what you want and
> have a burning desire to possess it.

## Be a "practical dreamer"

*Practical dreamers* are those who put their dreams into action. They have always been and always will be the patternmakers of civilization. We who desire to accumulate riches should remember the real leaders of the world always have been people who harnessed and put into practical use, the intangible, unseen forces of unborn opportunity and have converted those forces (or impulses of thought) into sky-scrapers, cities, factories, airplanes, automobiles, better health care, and every form of convenience that makes life more pleasant.

Tolerance and an open mind are practical necessities of the dreamer of today. Those who are afraid of new ideas are doomed before they start. Never has there been a time more favorable to pioneers than the present. True, there is no wild and woolly west to be conquered, as in the days of the Covered Wagon, but there is a vast business, financial, and industrial world to be remolded and redirected along new and better lines.

In planning to acquire your share of the riches, let no one influence you to scorn the dreamer. To win the big stakes in this ever changing world, you must catch the spirit of the great pioneers of the past, whose dreams have given to civilization all that it has of value, the spirit which serves as the life-blood of our own country—your opportunity and mine to develop and market our talents. Let us not forget, Columbus dreamed of an Unknown world, staked his life on the existence of such a world, and discovered it! Copernicus, the great astronomer, dreamed of a multiplicity of worlds and revealed them! No one denounced him as "impractical" after he had triumphed. Instead, the world worshipped at his shrine, thus proving once more that *"Success requires no apologies, failure permits no alibis."*

---

"Success requires no apologies, failure permits no alibis."

---

If the thing you wish to do is right, and you believe in it, go ahead and do it! Put your dream across, and never mind what "they" say if you meet with temporary defeat, for "they," perhaps, do not know that *every failure brings with it the seed of an equivalent success.*

## Transmute desire to riches

Every human being who reaches the age of understanding the purpose of money wishes for it. Wishing will not bring riches. But desiring riches with a state of mind that becomes an obsession, then planning definite ways and means to acquire riches and backing those plans with persistence which does not recognize failure, will bring riches. The method by which *desire* for riches can be transmuted into its financial equivalent, consists of these six definite, practical steps:

1. Fix in your mind the exact amount of money you desire. It is not sufficient merely to say, "I want plenty of money." Be definite as to the amount.
2. Determine exactly what you intend to give in return for the money you desire. (There is no such reality as getting something for nothing.)

3. Establish a definite date when you intend to possess the money you desire.
4. Create a definite plan for carrying out your desire, and begin at once to put this plan into action.
5. Write out a clear, concise statement of the amount of money you intend to acquire, the time limit for its acquisition, what you intend to give in return for the money, and the plan through which you intend to accumulate it.
6. Read your written statement aloud, twice daily, once just before retiring at night, and once after arising in the morning. *As you read, see and feel and believe yourself already in possession of the money.*

Follow the instructions described in these six steps, especially Step 6.

You may complain that it is impossible for you to "see yourself in possession of money" before you actually have it. Here is where a *burning desire* will come to your aid. If you truly *desire* money so keenly that your desire is an obsession, you will have no difficulty in convincing yourself that you will acquire it. The object is to want money and to become so determined to have it that you *convince* yourself you will have it.

Only those who become *money conscious* ever accumulate great riches. Money consciousness means that the mind has become so thoroughly saturated with the desire for money, that one can see one's self already in possession of it.

---

Only those who become *money conscious* ever accumulate great riches.

---

This method for transmuting desire into riches was received from Andrew Carnegie, who began as an ordinary laborer in the steel mills but managed, despite his humble beginning, to make these principles yield him a fortune of considerably more than one hundred million dollars. Furthermore, the six steps recommended here were carefully scrutinized by Thomas A. Edison, who placed his stamp of approval upon them as being the steps essential not only for the accumulation of money, but also for the attainment of any definite goal.

The steps call for *no hard labor*. They call for *no sacrifice*. They do not require one to become ridiculous or credulous (naive). To apply them requires no great amount of education. But the successful application of these six steps does call for sufficient imagination to enable one to see and understand that accumulation of money cannot be left to chance, good fortune, and luck. One must realize that all who have accumulated great fortunes first did a certain amount of dreaming, hoping, wishing, *desiring*, and *planning* before they acquired money. You can never have riches in great quantities, *unless* you can work yourself into a white heat of *desire* for money and actually *believe* you will possess it.

## Advice from Mary Kay Ash

Mary Kay Ash, the founder of Mary Kay Cosmetics, attributed her success to the development of self-confidence and *faith* in herself and in all the people in her vast organization, which now consists of more than 250,000 independent beauty consultants worldwide.

Her sales career began twenty-five years earlier when she joined Stanley Home Products. She often commented that she was not at all successful during her first year and was ready to give up. This changed when she attended her first Stanley sales seminar. She reported:

There I saw this tall, svelte, pretty, successful woman crowned queen as a reward for being the best in a company contest, and I determined to be that queen the following year, which seemed impossible. However, I decided to go up and talk to the president and to tell him that I intended to be queen next year.

Mr. Beveridge didn't laugh at me, but looked me in the eye, held my hand and said: "Somehow I think you will." Those five words drove me and the next year I was queen.

Mary Kay preached and practiced that the first step in achieving success is to firmly believe that you are an excellent person who deserves success. In an article in *Personal Excellence*, she suggested some exercises that will help you create your image of excellence and begin to establish an atmosphere of success in your life. Here are some of her suggestions:

- **Imagine yourself successful.** Always picture yourself successful. Visualize the person you desire to become. Set aside time each day to be alone and undisturbed. Get comfortable and relax. Close your eyes and concentrate on your desires and goals. See yourself in this new environment, capable, and self-confident.
- **Reflect on your past successes.** Every success, be it large or small, is proof that you are capable of achieving more successes. Celebrate each success. You can recall it when you begin to lose faith in yourself.
- **Set definite goals.** Have a clear direction of where you want to go. Be aware when you begin to deviate from these goals and take immediate corrective action.

- **Respond positively to life.** Develop a positive self-image. Your image, your positive reactions to life, and your decisions are completely within your control.

---

Imagine yourself successful, reflect on past successes, set definite goals, and respond positively to life.

---

## Stories of desire transmuted

The ability to transmute intangible desire into tangible riches and achievements is not fiction. Numerous individuals throughout history and in all fields of endeavor provide the proof that a definite, purposeful, burning desire coupled with planning and persistence is all that is required to achieve one's goals. You already read in Step 1 the story of Edwin C. Barnes, the man who *thought* his way into a partnership with Thomas A. Edison. His success began with a burning desire to work with Edison, not for him. In the following sections you can read the stories of other individuals who transmuted their intangible, burning desire into tangible success.

### Hernán Cortés sinks his own ships

In 1518, Spanish conquistador, Hernán Cortés set sail from Cuba to Mexico to conquer the Aztecs. Upon his arrival, he gave the order to sink the ships that had carried him and his men and supplies, sending a clear message that victory was the only option. There was no going back. They would win or perish.

With only about 500 men, some horses, and some cannons, Cortés was committed to winning. On his way, he visited other cities and met their people, other tribes that did not like their Aztec rulers. Cortés formed alliances with several tribes, including the powerful Tlaxcala who eventually helped Cortés lay siege to and conquer the city of Tenochtitlan (Mexico City) and with it the Aztec empire.

Every person who wins in any undertaking must be willing to sink his ships and cut all sources of retreat. Only by so doing can one be sure of maintaining that state of mind known as a *burning desire to win*, which is essential to success.

---

Committed to victory, Cortés removed all sources of retreat, leaving only two possible outcomes—victory or defeat. And, for him, defeat was not an option.

---

## Marshall Field rises from the ashes of the Great Chicago Fire

The morning after the Great Chicago Fire, a group of merchants stood on State Street, looking at the smoking remains of what had been their stores. They went into a conference to decide whether they would try to rebuild or leave Chicago and start over in a more promising area of the country. All except one reached a decision to leave Chicago.

The merchant who decided to stay and rebuild pointed a finger at the remains of his store and said, "Gentlemen, on that very spot I will build the world's greatest store, no matter how many times it may burn down." The store was built. It stands there today, a towering monument to the power of that state of mind known as a *burning desire*. The easy thing for Marshall Field to have done would have been exactly what his fellow merchants did. When the going was hard and the future looked dismal, they pulled up and went where the going seemed easier.

---

*When you have a burning desire,
no obstacle is too big to overcome.*

---

Mark well this difference between Marshall Field and the other merchants, because it is the same difference that distinguishes Edwin C. Barnes from thousands of other young men who have worked in the Edison organization. It is the same difference, which distinguishes practically all who succeed from those who fail.

## Stephen Spielberg wills his way onto the set

As a child, Steven Spielberg dreamed of being a movie director. He began making amateur films with a primitive camera when he was still a child, and his desire intensified.

How Spielberg broke into Universal Studios is a legend in the movie industry. He took the Universal Studios Tour, an attraction that enabled visitors to get an inside look at the movie business. Visitors ride around the studio lots on a tram. Steven sneaked off the tram and hid between two sound stages until the tour ended. When he left at the end of the day, he made a point to say a few words to the gate guard.

Day after day for three months, he returned to the studio. He walked past and waved at the guard, who waved back. He always wore a suit and carried a briefcase, letting the guard assume he was one of the summer interns. He spoke to and made friends with directors and writers and editors. He even found a vacant office, move in, and listed his name in the building directory.

He made it his business to get to know Sid Sheinberg, then head of production for the studio's television arm. He showed him his college film project, which so impressed Sheinberg that he put the young man under contract with the studio.

---

> Steven Spielberg is a person who had an idea, a distinct purpose, a *burning desire* to make it his reality, and the determination to follow through until he achieved his goal.

---

His first full-length film, *The Sugarland Express*, received critical acclaim and won a best-screenplay award at the 1974 Cannes Film Festival. Unfortunately, it performed poorly at the box office.

His big break came a year later when he came across the book *Jaws*. The studio had already decided to produce *Jaws* and had chosen a well-known director to film it.

Spielberg desperately wanted to make this movie. Despite the financial failure of *The Sugarland Express*, his self-confidence had not diminished, and he persuaded the producers to dismiss the chosen director and give the film to him.

It was not an easy assignment. From the beginning, trouble beset the production. It ran into technical problems and cost overruns. However, when *Jaws* was released in June 1975, it enjoyed twofold success: It broke box-office records, and the critics loved it. By the end of its theatrical run, it had earned about $260 million domestic and $210 million overseas for a total of nearly $470 million worldwide.

Over the next few years Spielberg directed several films that were not only box office successes but also critically acclaimed, including *Close Encounters of the Third Kind*, *Raiders of the Lost Ark*, *E.T. the Extra-Terrestrial*, *The Color Purple*, and *Lincoln*.

Spielberg continues to pursue his dreams. When he and two other Hollywood moguls created their own production company, they called it "Dreamworks."

## Practical dreamers overcome adversity

The world is filled with an abundance of *opportunity* which the dreamers of the past never knew. *A burning desire to be, and to do* is the launch pad. Dreams are not born of indifference, laziness, or lack of ambition. The world no longer scoffs at the dreamer, nor calls him impractical. Take courage, for these experiences have tempered the spiritual metal of which you are made—they are assets of incomparable value. Remember, too, that all who succeed in life get off to a bad start and pass through many heartbreaking struggles before they "arrive." The turning point in the lives of those who succeed usually comes at the moment of some crisis, through which they are introduced to their "other selves."

- **Henry Ford**, poor and uneducated, dreamed of a horseless carriage, went to work with what tools he possessed without waiting for opportunity to favor him, and now evidence of his dream is global. He has put more wheels into operation than anyone who ever lived, because he was not afraid to pursue his dreams.

- **Thomas Edison**, who started out as a part-time telegraph operator, dreamed of a lamp that could be operated by electricity, and despite more than ten thousand failures, he stood by that dream until he made it a physical reality. He failed innumerable times before he was driven, finally, to the discovery of the genius that slept within his brain.

- **Abraham Lincoln** dreamed of freedom for the black slaves, put his dream into action, and barely missed living to see a united North and South translate his dream into reality.

- **The Wright brothers** dreamed of a machine that would fly through the air. Now one may see evidence all over the world that they dreamed soundly.

- **Guglielmo Marconi** dreamed of a system for harnessing the intangible forces of the ether. Evidence that he did not dream in vain, may be found in every radio, TV, and cell phone in the world. His dream made the people of every nation on earth neighbors. It created a medium where news, information, and entertainment were broadcast around the world. It may interest you to know that Marconi's "friends" had him taken into custody and examined in a psychiatric hospital, when he announced he had discovered a principle through which he could send messages through the air, without the aid of wires or other direct physical means of communication.

- **John Bunyan** wrote the *Pilgrim's Progress*, which is among the finest of all English literature, after he had been confined in prison and sorely punished, because of his views on the subject of religion.

- **O. Henry** discovered the genius that slumbered in his brain only after he had met with great misfortune and was confined in a prison cell in Columbus, Ohio. Being forced, through misfortune, to become acquainted with his "other self," and to use his imagination, he discovered himself to be a great author instead of a miserable criminal and outcast.

- **Charles Dickens** began by pasting labels on blacking pots. The tragedy of his first love penetrated the depths of his soul, and converted him into one of the world's truly great authors. That tragedy produced first *David Copperfield*, then a succession of other works that made this a richer and better world for all who read his books.

- **Helen Keller** became deaf, dumb, and blind shortly after birth. Despite her misfortune, she has written her name indelibly in the pages of the history of the great. Her entire life has served as evidence that no one ever is defeated until defeat has been accepted as a reality.

- **Robert Burns** was an illiterate country lad cursed by poverty, who grew up to be a drunkard. The world was made better for his having lived, because he clothed beautiful thoughts in poetry and thereby plucked a thorn and planted a rose in its place.

- **Booker T. Washington** was born in slavery, handicapped by race and color. Because he was tolerant, had an open mind at all times on all subjects, and was a *dreamer*, he left his lasting impression on the entire human race.

- **Lou Ferrigno** suffered severe hearing loss at the age of three due to an ear infection. Skinny, he fantasized about bulking up to become muscular like his comic book heroes. To achieve his goal, he started lifting weights at the age of 12. At six feet five inches and 21 years old, he became the tallest and youngest to win the "Mr. Universe" title. Eventually he landed the role as The Hulk in the TV series *The Incredible Hulk*, starred in over 20 feature films, and became an internationally renowned fitness trainer. He now consuls others on how to face one's fears and overcome obstacles.

- **Beethoven** was deaf and **Milton** was blind, but their names will last as long as time endures, because they dreamed and translated their dreams into organized thought.

---

> The turning point in the lives of those who succeed usually comes at the moment of some crisis, through which they are introduced to their "other selves."

---

Strange and varied are the ways of life, and stranger still are the ways of Infinite Intelligence, through which people are sometimes forced to undergo all sorts of punishment before discovering their own brains and their own capacity to create useful ideas through imagination. Practical dreamers *do not quit!*

## Desire outwits Mother Nature

As a fitting climax to this chapter, I wish to introduce one of the most unusual persons I have ever known. I first saw him a few minutes after he was born. He came into the world without any physical sign of ears, and the doctor admitted, when pressed for an opinion, that the child might be deaf and mute for life.

I challenged the doctor's opinion. I had the right to do so; I was the child's father. I, too, reached a decision and rendered an opinion, but I expressed the opinion silently, in the secrecy of my own heart. I decided that my son would hear and speak. Nature could send me a child without ears, but Nature could not induce me to accept the reality of the affliction. In my own mind I knew that my son would hear and speak. How? I was sure there must be a way, and I knew I would find it. I thought of the words of the immortal Emerson, "The whole course of things goes to teach us faith. We need only obey. There is guidance for each of us, and by lowly listening, we shall hear the right word."

The right word? *Desire*! More than anything else, I *desired* that my son should not be a deaf mute. From that desire I never receded, not for a second. Many years previously, I had written, "Our only limitations are those we set up in our own minds." For the first time, I wondered if that statement were true. Lying on the bed in front of me was a newly born child, without the natural equipment of hearing. Even though he might hear and speak, he was obviously disfigured for life. Surely, this was a limitation, which that child had not set up in his own mind. What could I do about it? Somehow I would find a way to transplant into that child's mind my own *burning desire* for ways and means of conveying sound to his brain without the aid of ears.

> More than anything else, I *desired* that my son should not be a deaf mute. From that desire I never receded, not for a second.

As soon as the child was old enough to cooperate, I would fill his mind so completely with a *burning desire* to hear, that Nature would, by methods of her own, translate it into physical reality. All this thinking took place in my own mind, but I spoke of it to no one. Every day I renewed the pledge I had made to myself not to accept that my son would be deaf and mute.

As he grew older and began to take notice of things around him, we observed that he had a slight degree of hearing. When he reached the age when children usually begin talking, he made no attempt to speak, but we could tell by his actions that he could hear certain sounds slightly. That was all I wanted to know! I was convinced that if he could hear, even slightly, he might develop still greater hearing capacity. Then something happened which gave me hope. It came from an entirely unexpected source. We bought a record player. When the child heard the music for the first time, he became ecstatic and promptly appropriated the machine. He soon showed a preference for certain records, among them *It's a Long Way to Tipperary*. On one occasion, he played that piece over and over for almost two hours, standing in front of the record player with his teeth clamped on the edge of the case. The significance of this self-formed habit of his did not become clear to us until years afterward, for we had never heard of the principle of "bone conduction" of sound at that time.

Shortly after he appropriated the record player, I discovered that he could hear me quite clearly when I spoke with my lips touching his mastoid bone, or at the base of the brain. These discoveries placed in my possession the necessary media by which I began to translate into reality my *burning desire* to help my son develop hearing and speech. By that time he tried speaking certain words. The outlook was far from encouraging, but *desire backed by faith* knows no such word as "impossible."

Having determined that he could hear the sound of my voice plainly, I began, immediately, to transfer to his mind the desire to hear and speak. I soon discovered that the child enjoyed bedtime stories, so I went to work creating stories designed to develop in him self-reliance, imagination, and a keen desire to hear and to be normal.

---

*Desire* backed by *faith* knows no such word as "impossible."

---

There was one story in particular, which I emphasized by giving it some new and dramatic coloring each time it was told. It was designed to plant in his mind the thought that his affliction was not a liability, but an asset of great value.

Despite the fact that all the philosophy I had examined clearly indicated that *every adversity brings with it the seed of an equivalent advantage*, I must confess that I had not the slightest idea how this affliction could ever become an asset. However, I continued my practice of wrapping that philosophy in bedtime stories, hoping the time would come when he would find some plan by which his handicap could be made to serve some useful purpose.

---

*Every adversity brings with it the seed of an equivalent advantage.*

---

Reason told me plainly, that there was no adequate compensation for the lack of ears and natural hearing equipment. *Desire* backed by *faith* pushed reason aside and inspired me to carry on.

As I analyze the experience in retrospect, I can see now that my son's faith in me had much to do with the astounding results. He did not question anything I told him. I sold him the idea that he had a distinct advantage over his older brother and that this advantage would reflect itself in many ways. For example, the teachers in school would observe that he had no ears, and, because of this, they would show him special attention and treat him with extraordinary kindness. They always did. His mother saw to that by visiting the teachers and arranging with them to give the child the extra attention necessary. I sold him the idea, too, that when he became old enough to sell newspapers (his older brother had already become a newspaper merchant), he would have a big advantage over his brother, for the reason that people would pay him extra money for his wares, because they could see that he was a bright, industrious boy, despite the fact he had no ears.

We could notice that, gradually, the child's hearing was improving. Moreover, he had not the slightest tendency to be self-conscious because of his affliction. When he was about seven, he showed the first evidence that our method of servicing his mind was bearing fruit. For several months he begged for the privilege of selling newspapers, but his mother would not give her consent. She was afraid that his deafness made it unsafe for him to go on the street alone.

Finally, he took matters in his own hands. One afternoon, when he was left at home with the servants, he climbed through the kitchen window, shinned to the ground, and set out on his own. He borrowed six cents in capital from the neighborhood shoemaker, invested it in papers, sold out, reinvested, and kept repeating until late in the evening. After balancing his accounts and paying back the six cents he had borrowed from his banker, he had a net profit of forty-two cents. When we got home that night, we found him in bed asleep, with the money tightly clenched in his hand.

His mother opened his hand, removed the coins, and cried. Of all things! Crying over her son's first victory seemed so inappropriate. My reaction was the reverse. I laughed heartily, for I knew that my endeavor to plant in the child's mind an attitude of faith in himself had been successful.

---

*My endeavor to plant in the child's mind an attitude of faith in himself had been successful.*

---

His mother saw, in his first business venture, a little deaf boy who had gone out in the streets and risked his life to earn money. I saw a brave, ambitious, self-reliant little businessman whose stock in himself had been increased a hundred percent, because he had gone into business on his own initiative and had won. The transaction pleased me, because I knew that he had given evidence of a trait of resourcefulness that would go with him all through life.

Later events proved this to be true. When his older brother wanted something, he would lie down on the floor, kick his feet in the air, cry for it, and get it. When the "little deaf boy" wanted something, he would plan a way to earn the money, then buy it for himself. He still follows that plan!

Truly, my own son has taught me that handicaps can be converted into stepping stones on which one may climb toward some worthy goal, unless they are accepted as obstacles and used as excuses.

The little deaf boy went through the grades, high school, and college without being able to hear his teachers, except when they shouted loudly at close range. He did not go to a school for the deaf. We would not permit him to learn sign language. We were determined that he should live a normal life and associate with children in the general population, and we stood by that decision, although it cost us many heated debates with school officials.

While he was in high school, he tried an electrical hearing aid, but it was of no value to him. We believed this was due to a condition that was disclosed when the child was six. Dr. J. Gordon Wilson of Chicago operated on one side of the boy's head, and discovered that there was no sign of natural hearing equipment.

During his last week in college, (eighteen years after the operation), something happened which marked the most important turning point of his life. Through what seemed to be mere chance, he came into possession of another electrical hearing device, which was sent to him on trial. He was slow about testing it, due to his disappointment with a similar device. Finally he picked the instrument up and carelessly placed it on his head, hooked up the battery, and lo! as if by a stroke of magic, his lifelong *desire for normal hearing became a reality!* For the first time in his life he heard practically as well as any person with normal hearing.

---

His lifelong *desire for normal hearing became a reality!*

---

"God moves in mysterious ways, His wonders to perform."

Overjoyed because of the changed world that had been brought to him through his hearing device, he rushed to the telephone, called his mother, and heard her voice perfectly. The next day he plainly heard the voices of his professors in class for the first time in his life! Previously he could hear them only when they shouted at short range. He heard the radio. He heard the talking pictures. For the first time in his life, he could converse freely with other people without the necessity of their having to speak loudly. Truly, he had come into possession of a changed world. We had refused to accept Nature's error, and by *persistent desire* we had induced Nature to correct that error through the only practical means available.

*Desire* had commenced to pay dividends, but the victory was not yet complete. The boy still had to find a definite and practical way to convert his handicap into an equivalent asset.

Hardly realizing the significance of what had already been accomplished, but intoxicated with the joy of his newly discovered world of sound, he wrote a letter to the manufacturer of the hearing aid, enthusiastically describing his experience. Something in his letter—something, perhaps, which was not written in the lines, but between them—prompted the company to invite him to New York. When he arrived, he was escorted through the factory, and while talking with the Chief Engineer, telling him about his changed world, a hunch, an idea, or an inspiration—call it what you wish—flashed into his mind. It was this impulse of thought that converted his affliction into an asset destined to pay dividends in both money and happiness to thousands for all time to come.

---

By *persistent desire* we had induced Nature to correct that error through the only practical means available.

---

The sum and substance of that impulse of thought was this: it occurred to him that he might be of help to the millions of deaf people who go through life without the benefit of hearing devices, if he could find a way to tell them the story of his changed world. Then and there, he reached a decision to devote the remainder of his life to rendering useful service to the hard of hearing. For an entire month, he carried on intensive research. He analyzed the entire marketing system of the manufacturer of the hearing device and created ways and means of communicating with the hard of hearing all over the world for the purpose of sharing with them his newly discovered changed world. When this was done, he wrote a two-year plan, based upon his findings. When he presented the plan to the company, he was instantly given a position for the purpose of carrying out his ambition. Little did he dream, when he went to work, that he was destined to bring hope and practical relief to thousands of deaf people who, without his help, would have been doomed forever to deaf mutism.

Shortly after he became associated with the manufacturer of his hearing aid, he invited me to attend a class conducted by his company for the purpose of teaching the deaf and mute to hear and to speak. I had never heard of such a form of education, so I visited the class skeptical but hopeful that my time would not be entirely wasted. Here I saw a demonstration of what I had done to arouse and keep alive in my son's mind the *desire* for normal hearing. I saw the hearing impaired actually being taught to hear and to speak, through application of the self-same principle I had used, more than twenty years previously, in helping my own son.

Thus, through some strange turn of the Wheel of Fate, my son, Blair, and I had been destined to aid in correcting deaf mutism for those as yet unborn. We are the only living human beings, as far as I know, who have established definitely the fact that deaf mutism can be corrected to the extent of restoring to normal life those who have this affliction. It has been done for one; it will be done for others. There is no doubt in my mind that Blair would have been deaf and mute all his life if his mother and I had not managed to shape his mind as we did.

When Blair was an adult, Dr. Irving Voorhees, a noted specialist on such cases, examined him very thoroughly. He was astounded when he learned how well my son hears, and speaks, and said his examination indicated that "theoretically, the boy should not be able to hear at all." But the lad does hear, despite the fact that X-ray pictures show there is no opening in the skull, whatsoever, from where his ears should be to the brain.

When I planted in his mind the *desire* to hear and speak, that impulse carried with it some strange influence that caused Nature to become bridge-builder and span the gulf of silence between his brain and the outer world, by some means which the keenest medical specialists have been unable to interpret. It would be sacrilege for me to even conjecture as to how Nature performed this miracle. It would be unforgivable if I neglected to tell the world as much as I know of the humble part I assumed in the strange experience. It is my duty, and a privilege to say I believe, and not without reason, that nothing is impossible to the person who backs *desire* with enduring *faith*.

---

**Nothing is impossible to the person who backs *desire* with enduring *faith*.**

---

I have no doubt that a *burning desire* has devious ways of transmuting itself into its physical equivalent. Blair *desired* normal hearing; now he has it! He was born with a handicap, which might easily have sent one with a less defined desire to the street with a bundle of pencils and a tin cup. That handicap now promises to serve as the medium by which he will render useful service to many millions of hard of hearing, as well as to give him useful employment at adequate financial compensation for the remainder of his life. The little "white lies" I planted in his mind when he was a child, by leading him to *believe* his affliction would become a great asset, which he could capitalize, have been justified. There is nothing right or wrong that *belief* plus *burning desire* cannot make real. These qualities are free to everyone.

In all my experience in dealing with men and women who had personal problems, I never handled a single case that more definitely demonstrates the power of *desire*. Authors sometimes make the mistake of writing of subjects of which they have but superficial or very elementary knowledge. It has been my good fortune to have had the privilege of testing the soundness of the *power of desire* through the affliction of my own son. Perhaps it was providential that the experience came as it did, for surely no one is better prepared than he to serve as an example of what happens when *desire* is put to the test. If Mother Nature bends to the will of desire, is it logical that mere men can defeat a burning desire? Strange and imponderable is the power of the human mind! We do not understand the method by which it uses every circumstance, every individual, every physical thing within its reach as a means of transmuting *desire* into its physical counterpart. Perhaps science will uncover this secret.

The modus operandi by which this astounding result was achieved is not hard to describe. It consisted of three very definite facts:

1. I mixed *faith* with the *desire* for normal hearing, which I passed on to my son.
2. I communicated my desire to him in every conceivable way available, through persistent, continuous effort, over a period of years.
3. He believed me!

Several years ago, one of my business associates became ill. He became worse as time went on and finally was taken to the hospital for an operation. Just before he was wheeled into the operating room, I took a look at him and wondered how anyone as thin and emaciated as he could possibly go through a major operation successfully. The doctor warned me that there was little if any chance of my ever seeing him alive again. But that was the *doctor's opinion*. It was not the opinion of the patient. Just before he was wheeled away, he whispered feebly, "Do not be disturbed, Chief, I will be out of here in a few days."

The attending nurse looked at me with pity. But the patient did come through safely. After it was all over, his physician said, "Nothing but his own desire to live saved him. He never would have pulled through if he had not refused to accept the possibility of death." I believe in the power of *desire* backed by *faith*, because I have seen this power lift people from lowly beginnings to places of power and wealth; I have seen it rob the grave of its victims; I have seen it serve as the medium by which people staged a comeback after having been defeated in a hundred different ways; I have seen it provide my own son with a normal, happy, successful life, despite Nature's having sent him into the world without ears.

How can one harness and use the power of *desire?* This has been answered through this and the subsequent chapters of this book.

---

All achievement, no matter what its nature or purpose, begins with a *burning desire* for something definite. Through some strange and powerful principle of "mental chemistry" nature wraps up in the impulse of *strong desire* "that something" which recognizes no such word as "impossible" and accepts no such reality as failure.

---

## Expect it

Before passing to the next step, kindle anew in your mind the fire of hope, faith, courage, and tolerance. If you have these states of mind, and a working knowledge of the principles described, all else that you need will come to you, when you are *ready* for it. Let Emerson state the thought in these words:

Every proverb, every book, every byword that belongs to thee for aid and comfort shall surely come home through open or winding passages. Every friend whom not thy fantastic will, but the great and tender soul in thee craveth, shall lock thee in his embrace.

There is a difference between *wishing* for a thing and being *ready* to receive it. No one is ready for a thing, until he believes he can acquire it. The state of mind must be *belief*, not mere hope or wish. Open-mindedness is essential for belief. Closed minds do not inspire faith, courage, and belief.

---

No more effort is required to demand abundance and prosperity than is required to accept misery and poverty.

---

Remember, no more effort is required to aim high in life, to demand abundance and prosperity, than is required to accept misery and poverty. A great poet has correctly stated this universal truth through these lines:

*I bargained with Life for a penny*
*And Life would pay no more,*
*However I begged at evening*
*When I counted my scanty store.*

*For Life is a just employer,*
*He gives you what you ask,*
*But once you have set the wages,*
*Why, you must bear the task.*

*I worked for a menial's hire,*
*Only to learn, dismayed,*
*That any wage I had asked of Life,*
*Life would have willingly paid.*

The subconscious mind transmutes emotionally charged thought mixed with faith into it physical equivalent.

The subconscious mind works day and night.

The subconscious acts on the thoughts it is fed, whether they are positive or negative.

# Step 6

# Stamp Positive Impressions on Your Subconscious Mind

The human brain has three minds, which can be likened to activity centers:

- **Conscious:** The conscious mind filters (input and output), thinks, and reasons. It is the analytical part of the brain; as such, it has the power to determine whether certain information is true or false, to be accepted as belief or rejected. The conscious mind also provides the willpower to overcome emotional urges that arise from the subconscious mind.
- **Subconscious:** The subconscious mind records and classifies all sensory input, which may be recalled or withdrawn as letters from a filing cabinet. It is also where emotions are developed and is the source of emotional reactions, which may override or be overridden by ratio-

nal thinking and willpower. The subconscious is the home of behaviors and habits—the human equivalent of autopilot. It is the subconscious that serves as the gateway to Infinite Intelligence.

- **Unconscious:** The unconscious mind forms the automatic nervous system, which controls all involuntary bodily processes and functions, including breathing, heartbeat, digestion, and immune system response. Through deep hypnosis or meditation, one can influence the unconscious mind, as is evident through the use of biofeedback to control blood pressure, heartbeat, and chronic pain.

---

You cannot entirely control your subconscious mind, but you can voluntarily hand over to it any plan, desire, or purpose that you wish transformed into concrete form. The subconscious acts first on the dominating desires that have been mixed with emotional feeling, such as faith.

---

## The gateway to *Infinite Intelligence*

*The subconscious mind works day and night.* It draws upon the forces of Infinite Intelligence for the power to transmute one's desires into their physical equivalent, making use always of the most practical means by which this end may be accomplished.

It is the connecting link between the finite mind and Infinite Intelligence. It alone contains the secret process by which mental impulses are modified and changed into their spiritual equivalent. It alone is the medium through which prayer may be transmitted to the source capable of answering prayer. The possibilities of creative effort connected with the subconscious mind are stupendous, imponderable, and awe inspiring.

---

The subconscious mind is the connecting link between the finite mind and Infinite Intelligence.

---

I never approach the discussion of the subconscious mind without a feeling of humility and inferiority due, perhaps, to the fact that the entire stock of knowledge on this subject is so pitifully limited. The very fact that the subconscious mind is the medium of communication between the thinking mind and Infinite Intelligence is, of itself, a thought that almost paralyzes one's reason.

## Perform all 17 steps

After you have accepted as reality the existence of the subconscious mind and understand its possibilities as a medium for transmuting your *desires* into their physical or monetary equivalent, you begin to comprehend how the subconscious mind serves as a lynchpin for the 17 steps. Specifically, you begin to grasp the following:

- Everything that is created *begins* in the form of a thought impulse, as explained in Step 1. Nothing can be created that is not first conceived in *thought*.
- Every noteworthy achievement begins with a *burning desire* for what one wants, as stated in Step 5. You will also understand why *desires must be made clear and reduced to writing*.

- Through the process of autosuggestion, positive impressions may be made on the subconscious mind and be mixed with *faith*, as explained in Steps 6–8.
- Through the aid of the imagination (Steps 9–11), thought impulses may be assembled into plans. The imagination, when under control, may be used for the creation of plans or purposes that lead to the acquisition of one's object of desire or the achievement of one's goal. The mixing of faith with a plan or purpose intended for submission to the subconscious mind may be done *only* through the imagination.
- You must be persistent in carrying out instructions issued by the subconscious mind, as explained in Step 17.

---

Voluntary use of the subconscious mind calls
for coordination and application of all 17 steps.

---

Do not become discouraged if you do not succeed upon the first attempt. Be patient. Be persistent. You have not yet had time to master faith.

## Beware of negative thoughts

Remember, your subconscious mind acts on whatever belief and information it has, whether you make any effort to influence it or not. It will not remain idle! If you fail to plant *desires* in your subconscious mind, it will feed upon the thoughts that reach it as the result of your neglect. Thought impulses, both negative and positive, are reaching the subconscious mind continuously from the four sources that were mentioned in Step 11 on sex transmutation: Infinite intelligence, your own subconscious mind, another person's conscious thought, or another person's subconscious thought.

You are living in the midst of all manner of thought impulses that are reaching your subconscious mind without your knowledge. Some of these impulses are negative, some are positive. You are now engaged in trying to shut off the flow of negative impulses and to aid in voluntarily influencing your subconscious mind through positive impulses of *desire*.

When you achieve this, you will possess the key that unlocks the door to your subconscious mind. Moreover, you will control that door so completely that no undesirable thought may influence your subconscious mind.

> You are living in the midst of all manner of thought impulses that are reaching your subconscious mind without your knowledge.

## Thoughts are things

Ella Wheeler Wilcox, a famous poet and journalist of the late 19th and early 20th century, gave evidence of her understanding of the power of the subconscious mind when she wrote:

> *You never can tell what a thought will do*
> *In bringing you hate or love—*
> *For thoughts are things, and their airy wings*
> *Are swifter than carrier doves.*

*They follow the law of the universe—*
 *Each thing creates its kind,*
*And they speed o'er the track to bring you back*
 *Whatever went out from your mind.*

Ms. Wilcox understood the truth that thoughts which go out from one's mind also imbed themselves deeply in one's subconscious mind, where they serve as a magnet, pattern, or blueprint by which the subconscious mind is influenced while translating them into their physical equivalent. Thoughts are truly things, because every material thing begins in the form of thought-energy.

## Mixing thought impulses with emotion

The subconscious mind is more susceptible to influence by impulses of thought mixed with feeling or emotion than by those originating solely in the reasoning portion of the mind. In fact, much evidence supports the theory that *only* emotionalized thoughts have any *action* influence upon the subconscious mind. Emotion or feeling rules the majority of people. If it is true that the subconscious mind responds more quickly to and is influenced more readily by thought impulses that are well mixed with emotion, it is essential to become familiar with the more important of the emotions.

Emotions (or feeling impulses) may be likened to yeast in a loaf of bread, because they constitute the *action* element that transforms thought impulses from the passive to the active state. This is why thought impulses mixed with emotion are acted upon more readily than thought impulses originating in "cold reason."

You are preparing yourself to influence and control the "inner audience" of your subconscious mind, in order to hand over to it the *desire* for money, which you wish transmuted into its monetary equivalent. It is essential, therefore, that you understand the method of approach to this "inner audience." You must speak its language, or it will not heed your call. It understands best the language of emotion or feeling. Let us, therefore describe here the seven major positive emotions and the seven major negative emotions, so that you may draw upon the positives and avoid the negatives when giving instructions to your subconscious mind.

---

*Positive and negative emotions cannot occupy the mind at the same time*. One or the other must dominate. It is your responsibility to make sure that positive emotions constitute the dominating influence of your mind. Here the law of *habit* will come to your aid. *Form the habit* of applying and using the positive emotions! Eventually, they will dominate your mind so completely that the negatives *cannot enter it.*

---

Only by following these instructions literally, and continuously, can you gain control over your subconscious mind. The presence of a single negative in your conscious mind is sufficient to destroy all chances of constructive aid from your subconscious mind.

### The seven major positive emotions

These positive emotions must be injected, through the principle of autosuggestion (see Step 6), into the thought impulses that an individual wishes to pass on to the subconscious mind:

- Desire
- Faith
- Love
- Sex
- Enthusiasm
- Romance
- Hope

There are other positive emotions, but these are the seven most powerful, and the ones most commonly used in creative effort. Master these seven emotions (they can be mastered only by *use*), and the other positive emotions will be at your command when you need them.

### The Seven Major Negative Emotions (to be avoided)

The negatives voluntarily inject themselves into the thought impulses, which insure passage into the subconscious mind.

- Fear
- Jealousy
- Hatred
- Revenge
- Greed
- Superstition
- Anger

> Remember, in this connection, that you are studying a book that is intended to help you develop a "money consciousness" by filling your mind with positive emotions. *One does not become money conscious by filling one's mind with negative emotions.*

## Engaging in faith-based prayer

If you are an observing person, you must have noticed that most people resort to prayer *only* after everything else has *failed!* Or else they pray by a ritual of meaningless words. And, because it is a fact that most people who pray do so *only after everything else has failed*, they go to prayer with their minds filled with *fear* and *doubt*, which are the emotions the subconscious mind acts upon and passes on to Infinite Intelligence. Likewise, that is the emotion that Infinite Intelligence receives and *acts upon*.

If you pray for a thing but have fear as you pray that you may not receive it or that your prayer will not be acted upon by Infinite Intelligence, your prayer *will have been in vain.*

Prayer does, sometimes, result in the realization of that for which one prays. If you have ever had the experience of receiving that for which you prayed, go back in your memory and recall your actual *state of mind* while you were praying, and you will know for sure that the theory here described is more than a theory.

The time will come when the schools and educational institutions of the country will teach the "science of prayer." Moreover, prayer will be reduced to a science. When that time comes, (it will come as soon as humankind is ready for it and demands it), no one will approach the Universal Mind in a state of fear, for the very good reason that there will be no such emotion as fear. Ignorance, superstition, and false teaching will have disappeared, and we will have attained our true status as children of Infinite Intelligence. A few have already attained this blessing.

If you believe this prophesy is far-fetched, take a look at the human race in retrospect. Less than two hundred years ago, it was commonly believed that lightning was evidence of the wrath of God, and people feared it as such. Now, thanks to the power of *faith*, we have harnessed lightning and made it turn the wheels of industry. Until relatively recent times, it was believed that the space between the planets was nothing but a great void, a stretch of dead nothingness. Now, thanks to this same power of *faith*, we know that far from being either dead or a void, the space between the planets is very much alive, that it is the highest form of vibration known, excepting, perhaps, the vibration of *thought*. Moreover, we know that this living, pulsating, vibratory energy that permeates every atom of matter and fills every niche of space connects every human brain with every other human brain.

What reason do we have to believe that this same energy does not connect every human brain with Infinite Intelligence?

There are no tollgates between the finite mind of humans and Infinite Intelligence. The communication costs nothing except Patience, Faith, Persistence, Understanding, and a *sincere desire* to communicate. Moreover, the approach can be made only by each of us ourselves . Paid prayers are worthless. Infinite Intelligence does no business by proxy. You either go direct or you do not communicate.

You may buy prayer books and repeat them until the day of your doom, without avail. Thoughts that you wish to communicate to Infinite Intelligence must undergo transformation, such as can be given only through your own subconscious mind.

The method by which you may communicate with Infinite Intelligence is very similar to that through which the vibration of sound is communicated by wireless communication If you understand the working principle of radio, TV, and cellular phones, you know that audio and video cannot be communicated through the ether until it has been "stepped up," or changed into a rate of vibration which the human ear or eye cannot detect. The sending station picks up the audio and video and "scrambles" or modifies it by stepping up the vibration millions of times. Only in this way, can the vibrations be communicated through the ether. After this transformation has taken place, the ether "picks up" the energy and carries that energy to receiving stations, and these receiving sets "step" that energy back down to its original rate of vibration so it can be seen and heard.

The subconscious mind is the intermediary that translates one's prayers into terms that Infinite Intelligence can recognize, presents the message, and brings back the answer in the form of a definite plan or idea for procuring the object of the prayer. Understand this principle, and you will know why mere words read from a prayer book cannot and will never serve as an agency of communication between the human mind and Infinite Intelligence.

Before your prayer will reach Infinite Intelligence (a statement of the author's theory only), it probably is transformed from its original thought vibration into terms of spiritual vibration. Faith is the only known agency that will give your thoughts a spiritual nature. *Faith* and *fear* make poor bedfellows. Like light and darkness, where one is found, the other cannot exist.

Autosuggestion is the
only means to transfer
thoughts and beliefs to
the subconscious mind.

Your mind has no limitations
except those you choose to
acknowledge and accept.

Both poverty and riches
are the offspring of
thoughts planted in
the subconscious mind.

# Step 7

# Control Your Own Thoughts with Autosuggestion

*Autosuggestion* is the conscious repetition of emotion-charged affirmations or instructions to establish them as fact in the subconscious mind. Faith is the most powerful emotion, so repeating affirmations or instructions in a state of mind that sincerely believes them is the most effective way to transfer those beliefs to the subconscious mind.

---

*No thought, whether negative or positive, can enter the subconscious mind without the aid of the principle of autosuggestion, with the exception of thoughts picked up from the ether.*

---

The conscious faculty serves as an outer guard to the approach of the subconscious. All sense impressions perceived through the five senses are stopped by the *conscious*, thinking mind and may be either passed on to the subconscious mind or rejected at will. By nature, we have *absolute control* over the material that reaches our subconscious mind through our five senses. We rarely exercise this control, which explains why so many people go through life in poverty.

The subconscious mind is a fertile garden in which weeds will grow in abundance if the seeds of more desirable crops are not sown therein. *Autosuggestion* enables you to plant creative thoughts or, by neglect, permit thoughts of a destructive nature to be sown.

Many philosophers claim that people control their own earthly destinies, but most of them have failed to identify what gives people this control. The reason that one may control one's own earthly status, and especially one's financial status, is thoroughly explained in this chapter.

---

People may gain control of themselves and their environment, because they have the *power to influence their own subconscious minds* and through their subconscious minds gain the cooperation of Infinite Intelligence.

---

## Plant thoughts in your subconscious mind

To plant thoughts in your subconscious mind, take these six steps that were introduced in Step 5, "Develop a Burning Desire." To get satisfactory results, you must follow *all* instructions in a spirit of *faith* (see Step 8 for more about faith).

1. **Fix in your mind the exact amount of money you desire.** Be definite as to the amount. Concentrate or fix your attention on that money, eyes closed, until you can *actually see* the physical appearance of the money. Your ability to use the principle of autosuggestion depends greatly upon your capacity to *concentrate* on a given *desire* until that desire becomes a *burning obsession*.
2. **Determine exactly what you intend to give in return for the money you desire.** What product or service will you offer? When visualizing the money you intend to accumulate (with closed eyes), see yourself rendering the service or delivering the merchandise you intend to give in return for this money. This is important!
3. **Establish a definite date when you intend to possess the money you desire.** Mark the date on your calendar and post the date in other locations you are likely to see it on a daily basis. For example, write it on a Post-It note and stick it on your refrigerator or the edge of your computer monitor.
4. **Create a definite plan for carrying out your desire and begin at once to put this plan into action.** See Step 14 for guidance on planning.
5. **Write out a clear, concise statement of the amount of money you intend to acquire, the time limit for its acquisition, what you intend to give in return for the money, and the plan through which you intend to accumulate it.** For example, suppose that you intend to accumulate $1,000,000 by the first of January, five years hence, that you intend to deliver personal services in return for the money in the capacity of a sales representative. Your written statement of your purpose may read as follows:

By the first day of January, 20, [year], I will have in my possession $1,000,000, which will come to me in various amounts from time to time during the interim.

In return for this money I will give the most efficient service of which I am capable, rendering the fullest possible quantity, and the best possible quality of service as a sales representative of [the service or merchandise you intend to sell].

I believe that I will have this money in my possession. My faith is so strong that I can now see this money before my eyes. I can touch it with my hands. It is now awaiting transfer to me at the time and in the proportion that I deliver the service I intend to render in return for it. I am awaiting a plan by which to accumulate this money, and I will follow that plan, when it is received.

6. **Go to a quiet spot (preferably alone in bed) where you will not be disturbed or interrupted, close your eyes, and repeat aloud your written statement of the amount of money you intend to accumulate, the time limit for its accumulation, and a description of the product or service you intend to give in return for the money.** *As you read, see and feel and believe yourself already in possession of the money.* Do this twice daily, once just before retiring at night, and once after arising in the morning. (You can read your statement aloud until you have it memorized.)

Carry out these instructions as though you were a small child. Inject into your efforts something of the *faith* of a child.

> With autosuggestion, you play a perfectly legitimate "trick" on your subconscious mind by making it believe, because you believe it, that you must have the amount of money you are visualizing, that this money is already awaiting your claim, that the subconscious mind must hand over to you practical plans for acquiring the money which is yours. Hand over the thought suggested to your *imagination* and see what your imagination can or will do to create practical plans for accumulating that money.

By following these instructions, you communicate the object of your *desire* directly to your *subconscious* mind in a spirit of absolute *faith*. Through repetition of this procedure, you voluntarily create thought habits that are favorable to your efforts to transmute desire into its monetary equivalent.

## Infuse your desire with faith

Plain, unemotional words do not influence the subconscious mind. You will get no appreciable results until you learn to reach your subconscious mind with thoughts, or spoken words that have been well emotionalized with *faith*, the sincere *belief* that you *will* receive the object of your *desire*.

Do not become discouraged, if you cannot control and direct your emotions the first time you try to do so. Remember, there is no such possibility as *something for nothing*. Ability to reach and influence your subconscious mind has its price, and you *must pay that price*. You cannot cheat, even if you desire to do so. The price of ability to influence your subconscious mind is everlasting persistence in applying the principles described here. You cannot develop the desired ability for a lower price. You alone must decide whether the reward for which you are striving ("money consciousness") is worth the price you must pay for it in effort.

---

**Remember:** The mere reading of the words is of *no consequence* unless you mix emotion with your words. If you repeat a million times the famous Emil Coué formula, "Day by day, in every way, I am getting better and better," without mixing emotion and *faith* with your words, you will experience no desirable results. Your subconscious mind recognizes and acts upon *only* thoughts mixed with emotion. Failure to charge autosuggestion with emotion is the main reason the majority of people who attempt autosuggestion do not get the desired results.

---

Wisdom and cleverness alone will not attract and retain money except in a few very rare instances, where the law of averages favors the attraction of money through these sources. The method of attracting money described here does not depend upon the law of averages. Moreover, the method plays no favorites. It will work for one person as effectively as it will for another. Where failure is experienced, it is the individual, not the method, who has failed. If you try and fail, make another effort and still another until you succeed.

> **Remember:** The subconscious mind takes any orders given it in a spirit of absolute *faith*, and acts upon those orders, although the orders often have to be presented over and over again, through repetition, before they are interpreted by the subconscious mind.

## Create/receive plans

In the fourth of the six steps, you are instructed to "Create a definite plan for carrying out your desire and begin at once to put this plan into action." *Do not wait* for a definite plan, through which you intend to exchange services or merchandise in return for the money you are visualizing, but begin at once to see yourself in possession of the money, *demanding* and *expecting* meanwhile that your subconscious mind will hand over the plan(s) you need. Be on the alert for these plans and, when they appear, put them into *action immediately*. When the plans appear, they will probably "flash" into your mind through the sixth sense, in the form of an "inspiration." This inspiration may be considered a direct message from Infinite Intelligence. Treat it with respect and act upon it as soon as you receive it. Failure to do so will be *fatal* to your success.

> Do not trust to your reason (thinking mind) when creating your plan for accumulating money through the transmutation of desire. Reason is faulty. Moreover, your reasoning faculty may be lazy, and, if you depend entirely upon it to serve you, it may disappoint you.

## Be persistent

These instructions may, at first, seem abstract. Do not let this disturb or discourage you. Follow the instructions no matter how abstract or impractical they may, at first, appear to be. The time will soon come, if you do as you have been instructed, in spirit as well as in act, when a whole new universe of power will unfold to you. Skepticism, in connection with *all* new ideas, is characteristic of all human beings. But if you follow the instructions outlined, your skepticism will soon be replaced by belief, which will soon crystallize into *absolute faith*. Then you will have arrived at the point where you may truly say, "I am the master of my fate, I am the captain of my soul!"

---

You are now reading the chapter that represents the keystone to the arch of this philosophy. The instructions contained in this chapter must be understood and *applied with persistence*, if you succeed in transmuting desire into money.

---

After you have read the entire book, come back to this chapter, and follow in spirit and in action, this instruction:

Read the entire chapter aloud once every night, until you become thoroughly convinced that the principle of autosuggestion is sound, that it will accomplish for you all that has been claimed for it. As you read, underscore with a pencil every sentence that impresses you favorably.

Follow the foregoing instruction to the letter, and it will open the way for a complete understanding and mastery of the principles of success.

Faith is the visualization and belief in the attainment of desire.

To transmute *desire* for riches into *money,* you must first *convince* your subconscious mind that you *will* receive that money.

Autosuggestion convinces the subconscious mind to believe whatever you tell it to believe. It is the only method to induce faith.

# Step 8

# Believe It

*Faith* is the visualization and belief in the attainment of desire. It is the eternal elixir that gives life power and gives action to the impulse of thought! When *faith* is blended with the vibration of *thought*, the subconscious mind instantly picks up the vibration, translates it into its spiritual equivalent, and transmits it to Infinite Intelligence, as in the case of prayer.

The emotions of *faith*, *love*, and *sex* are the most powerful of all the major positive emotions. When the three are blended, they have the effect of coloring the vibration of thought in such a way that it instantly reaches the subconscious mind, where it is changed into its spiritual equivalent, the only form that induces a response from Infinite Intelligence.

Love and faith are psychic, related to the spiritual side of man. Sex is biological, but sexual desire can be transmuted from thoughts of physical expression to thoughts of another nature, as explained in Step 11. The mixing, or blending, of these three emotions has the effect of opening a direct line of communication between the finite, thinking human mind and Infinite Intelligence.

To think and grow rich, you must have faith in yourself and faith in the infinite:

- Faith is the starting point of all accumulation of riches!
- Faith is the basis of all miracles and all mysteries that cannot be analyzed by the rules of science!
- Faith is the only known antidote for failure!
- Faith mixed with prayer gives one direct communication with Infinite Intelligence.
- Faith transforms the ordinary vibration of thought, created by the finite mind of an individual, into the spiritual equivalent.
- Faith is the only agency through which the cosmic force of Infinite Intelligence can be harnessed and used.

---

Faith is the visualization and belief in the attainment of desire. It is the eternal elixir that gives life power and gives action to the impulse of thought!

---

## Induce faith through autosuggestion

*Faith* is a state of mind that may be induced (created) *autosuggestion*, by affirmation or repeated instructions to the subconscious mind, as explained in the next chapter. Autosuggestion "deceives" the subconscious mind into *believing* that you *will* receive that which you desire. For example, to transmute the intangible impulse of *desire* for riches into its physical counterpart, *money*, you *convince* your subconscious mind that you *will* receive that money. In return, your subconscious mind gives you faith followed by definite plans for procuring that which you desire.

1. Imagine the object of your desire. Any idea, plan, or purpose may be placed in the mind through repetition of thought.
2. Write a statement of your major purpose or *definite chief aim* and commit it to memory.
3. Repeat your statement of major purpose or *definite chief aim*, in audible words, day after day, until these vibrations of sound have reached your subconscious mind.
4. Conduct yourself just as you would if you are already in possession of the thing you desire.

Perfection comes through practice. It cannot come by merely reading instructions.

---

Repetition of affirmation to your subconscious mind is the only known method to induce faith.

---

## Nurture positive emotions and eliminate negative emotions

*The mind takes on the nature of the influences that dominate it.* Understand this truth, and you will know why it is essential for you to nurture positive emotions and eliminate negative emotions.

A mind dominated by positive emotions becomes a favorable abode for the state of mind known as *faith*. A mind so dominated may, at will, give the subconscious mind instructions, which it will accept and act upon immediately.

**Caution:** The subconscious mind will translate into its physical equivalent a thought impulse of a negative or destructive nature, just as readily as it will act upon thought impulses of a positive or constructive nature. This accounts for the strange phenomenon that so many millions of people experience, referred to as "misfortune" or "bad luck."

Millions of people *believe* themselves "doomed" to poverty and failure, because of some strange force over which they *believe* they have no control. They are the creators of their own "misfortunes," because of this negative *belief*, which is picked up by the subconscious mind and translated into its physical equivalent.

---

The law of autosuggestion, through which any person may rise to altitudes of achievement that stagger the imagination, is well described in the following verse:

If you *think* you are beaten, you are,
    If you *think* you dare not, you don't
If you like to win, but you *think* you can't,
    It is almost certain you won't.

If you *think* you'll lose, you're lost
    For out of the world we find,
Success begins with a person's will—
    It's all in the *state of mind*.

If you *think* you are outclassed, you are,
   You've got to *think* high to rise.
You've got to *be sure of yourself* before
   You can ever win a prize.

Life's battles don't always go
   To the stronger or faster man
But soon or late the one who wins
   Is the one who thinks he can!"

## Master the self-confidence formula

Resolve to throw off the influences of any unfortunate environment and build your own life to *order*. Taking inventory of mental assets and liabilities, you will discover that *your greatest weakness is lack of self-confidence*. This handicap can be surmounted, and timidity translated into courage, through the aid of the principle of autosuggestion. The application of this principle may be made through a simple arrangement of positive thought impulses stated in writing, memorized, and repeated, until they become a part of the working equipment of the subconscious faculty of your mind, as in the following *self-confidence formula*:

1. I know I have the ability to achieve the object of my definite purpose in life; therefore, I demand of myself persistent, continuous action toward its attainment, and I here and now promise to render such action.
2. I realize the dominating thoughts of my mind will eventually reproduce themselves in outward, physical action and gradually transform themselves into physical reality;

therefore, I will concentrate my thoughts for thirty minutes daily, upon the task of thinking of the person I intend to become, thereby creating in my mind a clear mental picture of that person.

3. I know through the principle of autosuggestion, any desire that I persistently hold in my mind will eventually seek expression through some practical means of attaining the object back of it; therefore, I will devote ten minutes daily to demanding of myself the development of self-confidence.
4. I have clearly written down a description of my definite chief aim in life, and I will never stop trying until I have developed sufficient self-confidence to attain it.
5. I fully realize that no wealth or position can long endure, unless built upon truth and justice; therefore, I will engage in no transaction that does not benefit all whom it affects. I will succeed by attracting to myself the forces I wish to use and the cooperation of other people. I will induce others to serve me by my willingness to serve others. I will eliminate hatred, envy, jealousy, selfishness, and cynicism by developing love for all humanity, because I know that a negative attitude toward others can never bring me success. I will cause others to believe in me, because I will believe in them and in myself.
6. I will sign my name to this formula, commit it to memory, and repeat it aloud once a day, with full faith that it will gradually influence my thoughts and actions so that I will become a self-reliant and successful person.

*Your greatest weakness is lack of self-confidence.*

Somewhere in your make-up (perhaps in the cells of your brain), there lies sleeping the seed of achievement that, if aroused and put into action, would carry you to heights such as you may never have hoped to attain.

Just as a master musician may cause the most beautiful strains of music to pour forth from the strings of a violin, so may you arouse the genius that lies asleep in your brain and cause it to drive you upward to whatever you wish to achieve.

## Let your faith resonate

Thoughts mixed with emotions constitute a "magnetic" force which attracts, from the vibrations of the ether, other similar, or related thoughts. A thought thus "magnetized" with emotion may be compared to a seed that, when planted in fertile soil, germinates, grows, and multiplies itself over and over again, until that which was originally one small seed, becomes countless millions of seeds of the *same kind*!

---

> Thoughts mixed with emotions constitute a "magnetic" force which attracts, from the vibrations of the ether, other similar, or related thoughts.

---

The ether is a great cosmic mass of eternal forces of vibration. It is made up of both destructive vibrations and constructive vibrations. It carries, at all times, vibrations of fear, poverty, disease, failure, and misery along with vibrations of prosperity, health, success, and happiness, just as surely as it carries, through the medium of radio, the sound of hundreds of orchestrations of music and hundreds of human voices, all of which maintain their own individuality and means of identification.

From the great storehouse of the ether, the human mind is constantly attracting vibrations that harmonize with that which *dominates* the human mind. Any thought, idea, plan, or purpose that one holds in one's mind attracts, from the vibrations of the ether, a host of its relatives, adds these "relatives" to its own force, and grows until it becomes the dominating, *motivating master* of the individual in whose mind it has been housed.

---

> We are what we are, because of the vibrations of thought that we pick up and register through the stimuli of our daily environment.

---

## Recognize the power of love

It is a known fact that the emotion of *love* is closely akin to the state of mind known as *faith*, and this for the reason that *love* comes very near to translating one's thought impulses into their spiritual equivalent. Careful analysis of the lifework and achievements of hundreds of men of outstanding accomplishment reveal the influence of a woman's love behind nearly *every one of them*. The emotion of love, in the human heart and brain, creates a favorable field of magnetic attraction that causes an influx of the higher and finer vibrations afloat in the ether.

---

> *Love* is closely related to the state of mind known as *faith* and comes very near to translating one's thought impulses into their spiritual equivalent.

Abraham Lincoln was a failure at everything he tried, until he was well past the age of forty. He was a Mr. Nobody from Nowhere, until a great experience came into his life and aroused the sleeping genius within his heart and brain, giving the world one of its really great men. That "experience" was mixed with the emotions of sorrow and *love*. It came to him through Anne Rutledge, the only woman whom he ever truly loved.

## Stories that demonstrate the power of faith

History contains numerous stories that demonstrate the power of faith in transforming intangible thought into tangible achievement. Here are just a few of those stories.

### Mahatma Gandhi shakes the foundation of the British Empire

Consider the power of *faith*, as it is was demonstrated by a man well known to all of civilization as Mahatma Gandhi. (In Sanskrit, "Mahatma" means "Great Soul.") In this man the world experienced one of the most astounding examples known to civilization of the possibilities of *faith*. Gandhi wielded more power than any person living in his time, despite the fact that he had none of the orthodox tools of power, such as money, soldiers, or armaments. He had no money, no home. He didn't even own a suit of clothes. But *he did have power*, enough power to win India's independence from the British Empire.

How did he come by that power? *He created it out of his understanding of the principle of faith and his ability to transplant that faith into the minds of two hundred million people.*

Gandhi accomplished, through the influence of *faith*, what the strongest military power on earth could not and never will accomplish through soldiers and military equipment. He accomplished the astounding feat of *influencing* two hundred million minds to *coalesce and move in unison, as a single mind*. What other force on earth except *faith* could do as much?

---

*Gandhi created power out of his understanding of the principle of faith and his ability to transplant that faith into the minds of two hundred million people.*

---

### Martin Luther King, Jr. leads the Civil Rights Movement

In the mid-20th century, Martin Luther King, through his deep faith and his belief in human rights and dignity for all people, led people of all races, religions, and beliefs to join in his struggle for civil rights. His dream that people will not be judged by the color of their skin but by the content of their character has not been fully realized, but his faith and his ability to transplant that faith in the minds of others led to significant progress in civil rights and served as an impetus to keep striving for its achievement.

### Charles M. Schwab wills the United States Steel Corporation into existence

Because of the need for faith and cooperation in operating business and industry, it is both interesting and profitable to analyze an event that provides an excellent understanding of the method by which industrialists and leaders of business accumulate great fortunes—by giving before they try to get.

The event chosen for this illustration dates back to 1900, when the United States Steel Corporation was being formed. As you read the story, keep in mind these fundamental facts and you will understand how *ideas* have been converted into huge fortunes:

1. Charles M. Schwab had an *idea* created through his *imagination*. The United States Steel Corporation was born in his mind before it actually came to *be*.
2. He mixed *faith* with his *idea*.
3. He formulated a *plan* for the transformation of his *idea* into physical and financial reality.
4. He put his plan into action with his famous speech at the University Club.
5. He applied and followed-through on his *plan* with *persistence* and backed it with firm *decision* until it had been fully carried out.
6. He prepared the way for success by a *burning desire* for success.

If you have any doubt that people can *think and grow rich*, this story should dispel that doubt, because you can plainly see in the story of the United States Steel Corporation the application of a major portion of the 17 steps described in this book.

---

The watchword of the future will be *human happiness and contentment*. When this state of mind is attained, the production will take care of itself more effectively than anything that has ever been accomplished where people did not and could not mix faith and individual interest with their labor.

---

John Lowell, in the *New York World-Telegram*, told this astounding description of the power of an *idea* and permitted it to be reprinted here.

### A pretty after-dinner speech for a billion dollars

When, on the evening of December 12, 1900, some eighty of the nation's financial nobility gathered in the banquet hall of the University Club on Fifth Avenue to do honor to a young man from out of the West, not half a dozen of the guests realized they were to witness the most significant episode in American industrial history.

J. Edward Simmons and Charles Stewart Smith, their hearts full of gratitude for the lavish hospitality bestowed on them by Charles M. Schwab during a recent visit to Pittsburgh, had arranged the dinner to introduce the thirty-eight-year-old steel man to eastern banking society. But they didn't expect him to stampede the convention. They warned him, in fact, that the bosoms within New York's stuffed shirts would not be responsive to oratory and that, if he didn't want to bore the Stilimans and Harrimans and Vanderbilts, he had better limit himself to fifteen or twenty minutes of polite vaporings and let it go at that.

Even John Pierpont Morgan, sitting on the right hand of Schwab as became his imperial dignity, intended to grace the banquet table with his presence only briefly. And so far as the press and public were concerned, the whole affair was of so little moment that no mention of it found its way into print the next day.

So the two hosts and their distinguished guests ate their way through the usual seven or eight courses. There was little conversation and what there was of it was restrained. Few of the bankers and brokers had met Schwab, whose career had flowered along the banks of the Monongahela, and none knew him well. But before the evening was over, they—and with them Money Master Morgan—were to be swept off their feet, and a billion dollar baby, the United States Steel Corporation, was to be conceived.

It is perhaps unfortunate, for the sake of history, that no record of Charlie Schwab's speech at the dinner ever was made. He repeated some parts of it at a later date during a similar meeting of Chicago bankers. And still later, when the Government brought suit to dissolve the Steel Trust, he gave his own version, from the witness stand, of the remarks that stimulated Morgan into a frenzy of financial activity.

It is probable, however, that it was a "homely" speech, somewhat ungrammatical (for the niceties of language never bothered Schwab), full of epigrams and threaded with wit. But aside from that it had a galvanic force and effect upon the five billions of estimated capital that was represented by the diners. After it was over and the gathering was still under its spell, although Schwab had talked for ninety minutes, Morgan led the orator to a recessed window where, dangling their legs from the high, uncomfortable seat, they talked for an hour more.

The magic of the Schwab personality had been turned on, full force, but what was more important and lasting was the full-fledged, clear-cut program he laid down for the aggrandizement of Steel. Many other men had tried to interest Morgan in slapping together a steel trust after the pattern of the biscuit, wire and hoop, sugar, rubber, whisky, oil or chewing gum combinations. John W. Gates, the gambler, had urged it, but Morgan distrusted him. The Moore boys, Bill and Jim, Chicago stockjobbers who had glued together a match trust and a cracker corporation, had urged it and failed. Elbert H. Gary, the sanctimonious country lawyer, wanted to foster it, but he wasn't big enough to be impressive. Until Schwab's eloquence took J. P. Morgan to the heights from which he could visualize the solid results of the most daring financial undertaking ever conceived, the project was regarded as a delirious dream of easy-money crackpots.

The financial magnetism that began, a generation ago, to attract thousands of small and sometimes inefficiently managed companies into large and competition-crushing combinations, had become operative in the steel world through the devices of that jovial business pirate, John W. Gates. Gates already had formed the American Steel and Wire Company out of a chain of small concerns, and together with Morgan had created the Federal Steel Company. The National Tube and American Bridge companies were two more Morgan concerns, and the Moore Brothers had forsaken the match and cookie business to form the "American" group—Tin Plate, Steel Hoop, Sheet Steel—and the National Steel Company.

But by the side of Andrew Carnegie's gigantic vertical trust, a trust owned and operated by fifty-three partners, those other combinations were picayune. They might combine to their heart's content but the whole lot of them couldn't make a dent in the Carnegie organization, and Morgan knew it.

The eccentric old Scot knew it, too. From the magnificent heights of Skibo Castle he had viewed, first with amusement and then with resentment, the attempts of Morgan's smaller companies to cut into his business. When the attempts became too bold, Carnegie's temper was translated into anger and retaliation. He decided to duplicate every mill owned by his rivals. Hitherto, he hadn't been interested in wire, pipe, hoops, or sheet. Instead, he was content to sell such companies the raw steel and let them work it into whatever shape they wanted. Now, with Schwab as his chief and able lieutenant, he planned to drive his enemies to the wall.

So it was that in the speech of Charles M. Schwab, Morgan saw the answer to his problem of combination. A trust without Carnegie—giant of them all—would be no trust at all, a plum pudding, as one writer said, without the plums. Schwab's speech on the night of December 12, 1900, undoubtedly carried the inference, though not the pledge, that the vast Carnegie enterprise could be brought under the Morgan tent. He talked of the world future for steel, of reorganization for efficiency, of specialization, of the scrapping of unsuccessful mills and concentration of effort on the flourishing properties, of economies in the ore traffic, of economies in overhead and administrative departments, of capturing foreign markets.

More than that, he told the buccaneers among them wherein lay the errors of their customary piracy. Their purposes, he inferred, had been to create monopolies, raise prices, and pay themselves fat dividends out of privilege. Schwab condemned the system in his heartiest manner. The shortsightedness of such a policy, he told his hearers, lay in the fact that it restricted the market in an era when everything cried for expansion. By cheapening the cost of steel, he argued, an ever-expanding market would be created; more uses for steel would be devised, and a goodly portion of the world trade could be captured. Actually, though he did not know it, Schwab was an apostle of modern mass production.

So the dinner at the University Club came to an end. Morgan went home, to think about Schwab's rosy predictions. Schwab went back to Pittsburgh to run the steel business for Andrew Carnegie, while Gary and the rest went back to their stock tickers, to fiddle around in anticipation of the next move.

It was not long coming. It took Morgan about one week to digest the feast of reason Schwab had placed before him. When he had assured himself that no financial indigestion was to result, he sent for Schwab—and found that young man rather coy. Mr. Carnegie, Schwab indicated, might not like it if he found his trusted company president had been flirting with the Emperor of Wall Street, the Street upon which Carnegie was resolved never to tread. Then it was suggested by John W. Gates the go-between, that if Schwab "happened" to be in the Bellevue Hotel in Philadelphia, J. P. Morgan might also "happen" to be there. When Schwab arrived, however, Morgan was inconveniently ill at his New York home, and so, on the elder man's pressing invitation, Schwab went to New York and presented himself at the door of the financier's library.

Now certain economic historians have professed the belief that from the beginning to the end of the drama, the stage was set by Andrew Carnegie—that the dinner to Schwab, the famous speech, the Sunday night conference between Schwab and the Money King, were events arranged by the canny Scot. The truth is exactly the opposite. When Schwab was called in to consummate the deal, he didn't even know whether "the little boss," as Andrew was called, would so much as listen to an offer to sell, particularly to a group of men whom Andrew regarded as being endowed with something less than holiness.

But Schwab did take into the conference with him, in his own handwriting, six sheets of copper-plate figures, representing to his mind the physical worth and the potential earning capacity of every steel company he regarded as an essential star in the new metal firmament.

Four men pondered over these figures all night. The chief, of course, was Morgan, steadfast in his belief in the Divine Right of Money. With him was his aristocratic partner, Robert Bacon, a scholar and a gentleman. The third was John W. Gates whom Morgan scorned as a gambler and used as a tool. The fourth was Schwab, who knew more about the processes of making and selling steel than any whole group of men then living. Throughout that conference, the Pittsburgher's figures were never questioned. If he said a company was worth so much, then it was worth that much and no more. He was insistent, too, upon including in the combination only those concerns he nominated. He had conceived a corporation in which there would be no duplication, not even to satisfy the greed of friends who wanted to unload their companies upon the broad Morgan shoulders. Thus he left out, by design, a number of the larger concerns upon which the Walruses and Carpenters of Wall Street had cast hungry eyes.

When dawn came, Morgan rose and straightened his back. Only one question remained. "Do you think you can persuade Andrew Carnegie to sell?" he asked.

"I can try," said Schwab.

"If you can get him to sell, I will undertake the matter," said Morgan.

So far so good. But would Carnegie sell? How much would he demand? (Schwab thought about $320,000,000). What would he take payment in? Common or preferred stocks? Bonds? Cash? Nobody could raise a third of a billion dollars in cash.

There was a golf game in January on the frost cracking heath of the St. Andrews links in Westchester, with Andrew bundled up in sweaters against the cold, and Charlie talking volubly, as usual, to keep his spirits up. But no word of business was mentioned until the pair sat down in the cozy warmth of the Carnegie cottage hard by. Then, with the same persuasiveness that had hypnotized eighty millionaires at the University Club, Schwab poured out the glittering promises of retirement in comfort, of untold millions to satisfy the old man's social caprices. Carnegie capitulated, wrote a figure on a slip of paper, handed it to Schwab and said, "All right, that's what we'll sell for."

The figure was approximately $400,000,000, and was reached by taking the $320,000,000 mentioned by Schwab as a basic figure, and adding to it $80,000,000 to represent the increased capital value over the previous two years.

Later, on the deck of a trans-Atlantic liner, the Scotsman said ruefully to Morgan, "I wish I had asked you for $100,000,000 more."

"If you had asked for it, you'd have gotten it," Morgan told him cheerfully.

The thirty-eight-year-old Schwab had his reward. He was made president of the new corporation and remained in control until 1930.

The dramatic story of "Big Business" which you have just finished was included in this book, because it is a perfect illustration of the method by which *desire can be transmuted into its physical equivalent!* I imagine some readers will question the statement that a mere, intangible *desire* can be converted into its physical equivalent. Doubtless some will say, "You cannot convert *nothing* into *something!*" The answer is in the story of the United States Steel Corporation. That giant organization was created in the mind of one man. The plan by which the organization was provided with the steel mills that gave it financial stability was created in the mind of the same man. His *faith,* his *desire,* his *imagination,* his *persistence* were the real ingredients that went into United States Steel. The steel mills and mechanical equipment acquired by the corporation, after *it had been brought into legal existence,* were incidental, but careful analysis will disclose the fact that the appraised value of the properties acquired by the corporation increased in value by an estimated six *hundred million dollars* by the mere transaction that consolidated them under one management.

---

> The United States Steel Corporation was created in the mind of one man.

---

In other words, Charles M. Schwab's *idea,* plus the *faith* with which he conveyed it to the minds of J. P. Morgan and the others, was marketed for a profit of approximately $600,000,000. Not an insignificant sum for a single *idea!* What happened to some of the people who took their share of the millions of dollars of profit made by this transaction is a matter with which we are not now concerned. The important feature of the astounding achievement is that it serves as unquestionable evidence of the soundness of the philosophy described in this book, because this philosophy was the warp and the woof of the entire transaction. Moreover, the practicability of the philosophy has been established by the fact that the United States Steel Corporation prospered and became one of the richest and most powerful corporations in America, employing thousands of people, developing new uses for steel, and opening new markets; thus proving that the $600,000,000 in profit which the Schwab *idea* produced was earned.

*Riches* begin in the form of *thought*! The amount is limited only by the person in whose mind the *thought* is put into motion. *Faith* removes limitations! Remember this when you are ready to bargain with Life for whatever it is that you ask as your price for having passed this way. Remember, also, that the man who created the United States Steel Corporation was practically unknown at the time. He was merely Andrew Carnegie's "Man Friday" until he gave birth to his famous *idea*. After that, he quickly rose to a position of power, fame, and riches.

---

*Riches* begin in the form of *thought*! The amount is limited only by the person in whose mind the *thought* is put into motion. *Faith* removes limitations!

---

*Imagination* is the workshop wherein all plans are fashioned.

Your only limitation, within reason, lies in the development and use of your imagination.

Ideas can be transmuted into cash through the power of definite purpose, plus definite plans.

Riches, when they come in huge quantities, are *never* the result of *hard work!*

# Step 9

# Engage Your Imagination

*Imagination* is the workshop wherein all plans are fashioned. The impulse or *desire* is given shape, form, and *action* through the aid of the imaginative faculty of the mind.

It has been said that one can create anything that he can imagine. Of all the ages of civilization, this is the most favorable for the development of the imagination, because it is an age of rapid change. On every hand one may contact stimuli that develop the imagination. Through the aid of his imaginative faculty, humankind has discovered and harnessed more of Nature's forces during the past hundred years than during the entire history of the human race, previous to that time. We have conquered the air so completely, that the birds are a poor match for us in flying. We have harnessed the ether and made it serve as a means of instantaneous communication with any part of the world. We have analyzed and weighed the sun at a distance of nearly 100 million miles and have determined, through the aid of *imagination*, the elements of which it consists. We have discovered that our own brain is both a broadcasting and a receiving station for the vibration of thought, and we are beginning now to learn how to make practical use of this discovery. We have increased the speed of locomotion, until we may now travel at a speed of more than six hundred miles an hour. We may breakfast in New York and lunch in San Francisco.

*Our only limitation*, within reason, *lies in the development and use of our imagination.* We have not yet reached the apex of development in the use of our imaginative faculty. We have merely discovered that we have an imagination and have commenced to use it in a very elementary way.

---

**Our only limitation, within reason, lies in the development and use of our imagination.**

---

Keep in mind as you follow these principles that the entire story of how one may convert *desire* into money cannot be told in one statement. The story will be complete, only when one has *mastered, assimilated,* and *begun to make use of all the principles.*

## Two forms of imagination

The imaginative faculty functions in two forms:

- **Synthetic imagination:** Through this faculty, one may arrange old concepts, ideas, or plans into new combinations. This faculty creates nothing. It merely works with what it is fed in the forms of experience, education, and observation. It is the faculty used most by the inventor, with the exception of the "genius" who draws upon the creative imagination when he cannot solve his problem through synthetic imagination.

- **Creative imagination:** Through the faculty of creative imagination, the finite mind of humankind has direct communication with Infinite Intelligence. It is the faculty through which "hunches" and "inspirations" are received. It is by this faculty that all basic or new ideas are developed. It is through this faculty that thought vibrations from the minds of others are received. It is through this faculty that one individual may "tune in," or communicate with the subconscious minds of others. The creative imagination works automatically and functions *only* when the conscious mind is vibrating at an exceedingly rapid rate as, for example, when the conscious mind is stimulated through the emotion of a strong desire.

Both the synthetic and creative faculties of imagination more alert, more receptive to vibrations from the sources mentioned, in proportion to their development through *use*, just as any skill or organ of the body develops through use. Your imaginative faculty may have become weak through inaction, but it can be revived and made alert through *use*. The great leaders of business, industry, finance, and the great artists, musicians, poets, and writers became great, because they developed the faculty of creative imagination.

Center your attention, for the time being, on the development of the synthetic imagination, because this is the faculty that you will use more often in the process of converting desire into money. However, in the process of transforming the impulse of *desire* into money, you may face circumstances and situations which demand use of the creative imagination as well.

Transformation of the intangible impulse, of *desire*, into the tangible reality, of *money*, calls for the use of a plan, or plans. These plans must be formed with the aid of the *imagination*, and mainly, with the *synthetic imagination*. Read the entire book through, then come back to this chapter, and begin at once to put your imagination to work on the building of a plan, or plans, for the transformation of your *desire* into money.

---

*Desire* is only a thought, an impulse. It is nebulous and ephemeral. It is abstract and of no value, until it has been transformed into its physical counterpart. Imagination builds the plan that transmutes desire into its physical counterpart. It builds the bridge between desire and the object of desire.

---

## How to develop your imagination

There are numerous ways to nurture creativity and develop your imagination. Here are a few you might want to try:

- **Read widely.** The more information you feed your synthetic imagination, the more it has to work with in organizing knowledge to formulate new ideas and plans. Reading from a variety of sources on a variety of topics expands the reach of your synthetic imagination.
- **Be curious, ask questions.** Curiosity is a symptom of a thirsty imagination. In addition, it is human nature's way of refusing to accept what one perceives without fully understanding it. The pursuit of answering questions often leads to deeper insight and creative solutions.

- **Expand your interests.** Another way to feed your synthetic imagination is to expand your interests. The specific knowledge you acquire through engagement in a hobby or desire to understand a topic may inform your imagination in a way that it invents a product or service relevant to your career. In addition, many people have built lucrative businesses around their interests or hobbies.
- **Travel.** Travel exposes you to different people, languages, world views, and ways of addressing problems or issues.
- **Converse with other creative people.** Sharing ideas with others in your *Master Mind group* is a way to tap the power of collective imagination, which may involve both synthetic and creative imagination. See Step 13 for more about the *Master Mind group*.
- **Take notes.** Record observations of anything that fills you with awe or wonder. The writing process not only reinforces the impressions on your mind but can often stimulate creative thought.
- **Retreat in nature.** Spend time in nature, either camping or going on nature walks to open your mind to universal consciousness. At least one study, by psychologists from the University of Utah and University of Kansas in 2012, shows that backpackers scored 50 percent higher on a creativity test after spending four days in nature.
- **Practice mindfulness.** Creativity occurs in the neocortex but only when the brain isn't preoccupied or overwhelmed with other concerns, such as emotional imbalances and survival concerns. Mindfulness and other meditation techniques calm other areas of the brain to

allow the neocortex to do its job. Several companies, including the Walt Disney Company, General Mills, and Google have implemented meditation programs to boost creativity in employees.

---

> As soon as you have a plan, reduce it to writing, if you have not already done so. The moment you complete this, you will have *definitely* given concrete form to the intangible *desire*. The moment you reduce the statement of your desire and your plan for its realization to writing, you have actually *taken the first* of a series of steps that will enable you to convert the thought into its physical counterpart.

---

## How to make practical use of imagination

Like knowledge, imagination must be applied in order to create something of value. In terms of thinking and growing rich, imagination can be applied to accomplish the following:

- **Devise plans.** The imagination is responsible for devising plans that transmute intangible desire into the acquisition of the object of that desire.
- **Overcome obstacles.** When obstacles are encountered, the imagination often delivers ways to overcome or work around those obstacles.
- **Solve problems.** Many of the most lucrative inventions are nothing more than imaginative solutions to problems.
- **Address unmet or underserved needs.** Unmet or underserved needs are goldmines for the imagination.

- **Identify opportunities.** Amazon.com founder Jeff Bezos spotted a golden opportunity when he realized that online ordering could be combined with shipping services to enable people to shop from home.

A properly nurtured imagination requires no extra effort on your part to devise plans or creative solutions. It does not require reason. All you need is a *thought*, defined in Step 1 as "a definite idea combined with purpose, persistence, burning desire, and faith." Your imagination will deliver the plan or solution.

## No hard work required

If you are one of those who believe that hard work and honesty alone will bring riches, perish the thought! It is not true! Riches, when they come in huge quantities, are never the result of *hard* work! Riches come, if they come at all, in response to definite demands, based upon the application of definite principles, and not by chance or luck.

Generally speaking, an idea is an impulse of thought that impels action by an appeal to the imagination. All master sales reps know that ideas can be sold where merchandise cannot. Ordinary sales reps do not know this-that is why they are "ordinary."

---

There is no standard price on ideas. The creator of ideas makes his own price and, if he is smart, gets it.

---

## Do not depend on favorable breaks or good luck

Millions of people go through life hoping for favorable "breaks." Perhaps a favorable break can get one an opportunity, but the safest plan is not to depend upon luck. It was a favorable "break" that gave me the biggest opportunity of my life; however, twenty-five years of determined effort had to be devoted to that opportunity before it became an asset.

The "break" consisted of my good fortune in meeting and gaining the cooperation of Andrew Carnegie. On that occasion Carnegie planted in my mind the idea of organizing the principles of achievement into a philosophy of success. Thousands of people have profited by the discoveries made in the twenty-five years of research, and several fortunes have been accumulated through the application of the philosophy. The beginning was simple. It was an *idea* that anyone might have developed.

The favorable break came through Carnegie, but what about the *determination, definiteness of purpose,* the d*esire to attain the goal,* and the *persistent effort of twenty-five years*? It was no ordinary *desire* that survived disappointment, discouragement, temporary defeat, criticism, and the constant reminder that my efforts were a "waste of time." It was a *burning desire,* an *obsession!*

When Mr. Carnegie first planted the idea in my mind, it was coaxed, nursed, and enticed to remain alive. Gradually, the idea became a giant under its own power, and it coaxed, nursed, and drove me. Ideas are like that. First you give life and action and guidance to ideas, and then they take on power of their own and sweep aside all opposition.

Ideas are intangible forces, but they have more power than the physical brains that give birth to them. They have the power to live on after the brain that creates them has returned to dust. For example, take the power of Christianity. That began with a simple idea born in the brain of Christ. Its chief tenet was, "Do unto others as you would have them do unto you." Christ has gone back from the source from whence He came, but His *idea* goes marching on. Someday, it may grow up and come into its own, then it will have fulfilled Christ's deepest *desire*. The idea has been developing only two thousand years. Give it time!

## Stories that reveal imagination at work

*Ideas* are *products of the imagination* and the starting points of all fortunes. Let us examine a few well-known ideas that have yielded huge fortunes. Perhaps these stories will provide the spark that ignites your imagination to conceive an innovation that you can use to start to accumulate riches.

### The enchanted kettle

Many years ago, an old country doctor drove to town, hitched his horse, quietly slipped into a drug store by the back door, and began "dickering" with the young pharmacy clerk. His mission was destined to yield great wealth to many people. It was destined to bring to the South the most far-flung benefit since the Civil War.

For more than an hour, behind the prescription counter, the old doctor and the clerk talked in low tones. Then the doctor left. He went out to the buggy and brought back a large, old-fashioned kettle and a big wooden paddle (used for stirring the contents of the kettle), and deposited them in the back of the store.

The clerk inspected the kettle, reached into his inside pocket, took out a roll of bills, and handed it over to the doctor. The roll contained exactly $500—the clerk's entire savings!

The doctor handed over a small slip of paper on which was written a secret formula. The words on that small slip of paper were worth a King's ransom! *But not to the doctor!* Those magic words were needed to start the kettle to boiling, but neither the doctor nor the young clerk knew what fabulous fortunes were destined to flow from that kettle.

The old doctor was glad to sell the outfit for $500. The money would pay off his debts and give him freedom of mind. The clerk was taking a big chance by staking his entire life's savings on a mere scrap of paper and an old kettle! He never dreamed his investment would start a kettle to overflowing with gold that would surpass the miraculous performance of Aladdin's lamp.

What the clerk really purchased was an *idea!*

The old kettle, the wooden paddle, and the secret message on the slip of paper were incidental. The strange performance of that kettle began to take place after the new owner mixed with the secret instructions an ingredient of which the doctor knew nothing.

Read this story carefully and give your imagination a test! See if you can discover what the young man added to the secret message that caused the kettle to overflow with gold. Remember, as you read, that this is not a story from Arabian Nights. Here you have a story of facts stranger than fiction, facts which began in the form of an *idea*.

Let us take a look at the vast fortunes of gold this idea has produced. It has paid and still pays huge fortunes to men and women all over the world, who distribute the contents of the kettle to millions of people.

The old kettle is now one of the world's largest consumers of sugar, thus providing jobs of a permanent nature to thousands of men and women engaged in growing sugar cane and refining and marketing sugar.

The old kettle consumes, annually, millions of plastic bottles and aluminum cans, providing jobs to huge numbers of workers in the bottling industry. The old kettle gives employment to an army of clerks, copy writers, and advertising experts throughout the nation. It has brought fame and fortune to scores of artists who have created magnificent pictures describing the product. The old kettle has converted a small Southern city into the business capital of the South, which now benefits, directly or indirectly, every business and practically every resident of the city. The influence of this idea now benefits every civilized country in the world, pouring out a continuous stream of gold to all who touch it.

Gold from the kettle built and maintains one of the most prominent colleges of the South, where thousands of young people receive the training essential for success.

The old kettle has done other marvelous things.

All through the depression of the 1930s, when factories, banks, and business houses were folding up and quitting by the thousands, the owner of this enchanted kettle went marching on, *giving continuous employment* to an army of men and women all over the world and paying out extra portions of gold to those who, long ago, *had faith in the idea.*

If the product of that old brass kettle could talk, it would tell thrilling tales of romance in every language: romances of love, romances of business, romances of professional men and women who are daily being stimulated by it.

The author is sure of at least one such romance, for he was a part of it, and it all began not far from the very spot on which the pharmacy clerk purchased the old kettle. It was here that the author met his wife, and it was she who first told him of the enchanted kettle. It was the product of that kettle they were drinking when he asked her to accept him "for better or worse."

Now that you know the content of the enchanted kettle is a world famous drink, it is fitting that the author confess that the home city of the drink supplied him with a wife, also that the drink itself provides him with stimulation of thought without intoxication and thereby serves to give the refreshment of mind which an author must have to do his best work.

Whoever you are, wherever you may live, whatever occupation you may be engaged in, just remember in the future, every time you see the words "Coca-Cola," that its vast empire of wealth and influence grew out of a single *idea*, and that the mysterious ingredient the drug clerk—Asa Candler—mixed with the secret formula was . . . *imagination!*

Stop and think about that for a moment.

Remember, also, that the thirteen steps to riches, described in this book, were the media through which the influence of Coca-Cola has been extended to every city, town, village, and crossroads of the world, and that *any idea* you may create, as sound and *meritorious* as Coca-Cola, has the possibility of duplicating the stupendous record of this worldwide thirst-killer.

Truly, thoughts are things, and their scope of operation is the world itself.

## What I would do if I had a million dollars

This story proves the truth of that old saying, "Where there's a will, there's a way." It was told to me by that beloved educator and clergyman, Frank W. Gunsaulus, who began his preaching career in the stockyards region of South Chicago.

While Dr. Gunsaulus was going through college, he observed many defects in our educational system, defects which he believed he could correct if he were the head of a college. His deepest desire was to become the directing head of an educational institution in which young men and women would be taught to "learn by doing."

He made up his mind to organize a new college in which he could carry out his ideas without being handicapped by orthodox methods of education. He needed a *million dollars* to bring the project to fruition. Where was he to lay his hands on so large a sum of money? That was the question that absorbed most of this ambitious young preacher's thought.

But he couldn't seem to make any progress.

Every night he took that thought to bed with him. He got up with it in the morning. He took it with him everywhere he went. He turned it over and over in his mind until it became a consuming obsession with him. A million dollars is a lot of money. He recognized that fact, but he also recognized the truth that the only limitation is that which one sets up in one's own mind.

Being a philosopher as well as a preacher, Dr. Gunsaulus recognized, as do all who succeed in life, that *definiteness of pur-*

*pose* is the starting point from which one must begin. He recognized, too, that definiteness of purpose takes on animation, life, and power when backed by a *burning desire* to translate that purpose into its material equivalent.

He knew all these great truths, yet he did not know where or how to lay his hands on a million dollars. The natural procedure would have been to give up and quit by saying, "Ah well, my idea is a good one, but I cannot do anything with it, because I never can procure the necessary million dollars." That is exactly what the majority of people would have said, but it is not what Dr. Gunsaulus said. What he said and did are so important that I now introduce him and let him speak for himself:

One Saturday afternoon I sat in my room thinking of ways and means of raising the money to carry out my plans. For nearly two years, I had been thinking, but I had done nothing but think!

The time had come for *action!*

I made up my mind, then and there, that I would get the necessary million dollars within a week. How? I was not concerned about that. The main thing of importance was the decision to get the money within a specified time, and I want to tell you that the moment I reached a definite decision to get the money within a specified time, a strange feeling of assurance came over me, such as I had never before experienced. Something inside me seemed to say, "Why didn't you reach that decision a long time ago? The money was waiting for you all the time!" Things began to happen in a hurry. I called the newspapers and announced I would preach a sermon the following morning entitled, "What I would do if I had a million dollars."

I went to work on the sermon immediately, but I must tell you frankly the task was not difficult, because I had been preparing that sermon for almost two years. The spirit behind it was a part of me!

Long before midnight I had finished writing the sermon. I went to bed and slept with a feeling of confidence, for *I could see myself already in possession of the million dollars.*

Next morning I arose early, went into the bathroom, read the sermon, then knelt and prayed that my sermon might come to the attention of someone who would supply the needed money.

While I was praying, I again had that feeling of assurance that the money would be forthcoming. In my excitement, I walked out without my sermon and did not discover the oversight until I was in my pulpit and about ready to begin delivering it.

It was too late to go back for my notes, and what a blessing that I couldn't go back! Instead, my own subconscious mind yielded the material I needed. When I arose to begin my sermon, I closed my eyes and spoke with all my heart and soul of my dreams. I not only talked to my audience, but I fancy I talked also to God. I told what I would do with a million dollars if that amount were placed in my hands. I described the plan I had in mind for organizing a great educational institution, where young people would learn to do practical things and at the same time develop their minds.

When I had finished and sat down, a man slowly arose from his seat, about three rows from the rear, and made his way toward the pulpit. I wondered what he was going to do. He came into the pulpit, extended his hand, and said, "Reverend, I liked your sermon. I believe you can do everything you said you would if you had a million dollars. To prove that I believe in you and your sermon, if you will come to my office tomorrow morning, I will give you the million dollars. My name is Phillip D. Armour."

Young Gunsaulus went to Mr. Armour's office, and the million dollars was presented to him. With the money, he founded the Armour Institute of Technology. That is more money than the majority of preachers ever see in an entire lifetime, yet the thought impulse behind the money was created in the young preacher's mind in a fraction of a minute. The necessary million dollars came as a result of an idea served up by imagination. Behind the idea was a *desire* that young Gunsaulus had been nursing in his mind for almost two years.

---

**Observe this important fact:** *Gunsaulus got the money within thirty-six hours after he reached a definite decision in his own mind to get it and decided upon a definite plan for getting it!*

---

There was nothing new or unique about young Gunsaulus' vague thinking about a million dollars and weakly hoping for it. Others before him, and many since his time, have had similar thoughts. But there was something very unique and different about the decision he reached on that memorable Saturday, when he put vagueness into the background and definitely said, "I *will* get that money within a week!"

---

God seems to throw Himself on the side of people who know exactly what they want, if they are determined to get *just that!*

---

Moreover, the principle through which Dr. Gunsaulus got his million dollars is still alive! It is available to you! This universal law is as workable today as it was when the young preacher made use of it so successfully. This book describes, step by step, the thirteen elements of this great law and suggests how they may be put to use.

Observe that Asa Candler and Dr. Frank Gunsaulus had one characteristic in common. Both knew the astounding truth that *ideas can be transmuted into cash through the power of definite purpose, plus definite plans.*

## Herb Kelleher, seller of ideas

The story of practically every great fortune starts with the day when a creator of ideas and a seller of ideas got together and worked in harmony. Herb Kelleher, one of the founders of Southwest Airlines, is a good example of a "seller of ideas." He was a lawyer in San Antonio, Texas when Rollin King, the creator of an idea, asked for his help in founding a new airline.

Rollin King was an investment adviser. As a side business, he ran an unprofitable air charter service between small Texas cities. At that time, most Americans who traveled by air were business executives or wealthy pleasure seekers. King was frustrated when he wanted to fly from one city in Texas to another. He could never get a seat on the airlines that currently flew those routes—besides, prices were too high.

He recognized the need to create an airline that would fly just between the three biggest cities in the state, but King knew his little airline wasn't up to the task so he decided to start one. He put together a feasibility study and business plan. He raised $100,000 in pocket money and then went to Herb Kelleher, his lawyer, to arrange for the necessary paperwork to create Air Southwest Co. (later Southwest Airlines Co.).

Although Kelleher was at first skeptical, he worked with King to gain additional capital and some political support. On Feb. 20, 1968, the Texas Aeronautics Commission approved Southwest's petition to fly between the three cities. However, on Feb. 21, competing airlines—Braniff, Trans Texas, and Continental—blocked the approval with a temporary restraining order.

Kelleher, his enthusiasm for the airline ignited by the efforts to quash it, put his litigation skills to work. The competition argued that Texas didn't need a new carrier. It took a three-and-a-half-year legal battle, including three trips to three courts, for Southwest to prove otherwise, and Southwest was granted the necessary permission and started operating.

Although they made a good start, it wasn't enough. The company lost $3.7 million that year, and the losses continued for another year and a half. Southwest was trying to keep costs down and attract customers without compromising its original goals.

By this time Kelleher had become so enthralled with the concept that he gave up his law practice to run Southwest. His aim was to make Southwest the airline of choice in the market it served.

One of his innovations was peak and off-peak airline pricing. Another was the 10-minute turn-around. After landing, each plane would pull into the gate, get checked by maintenance, unload passengers, reload, and leave the gate within 10 minutes instead of the 45 minutes other airlines took. The 10-minute turnaround allowed the three-plane airline to maintain a busy schedule and improve its on-time performance.

Because of their very limited budget, they couldn't advertise in the usual media, so they chose to promote the airline by word of mouth. To do this company decided to cultivate a sensational, off-the-wall image.

Customer service became their top priority. Flight attendants were trained to give "tender loving care" to the passengers. The company's slogan: "Now there's somebody else up there who loves you."

In addition, Kelleher, eliminated the annoying, time consuming methods the major airlines used in issuing boarding passes, By creating open-seating on all flights, no seat reservations were needed and passengers were given numbered boarding cards which were issued and collected at the gate.

With the passenger satisfaction as its main objective, Kelleher and his team built up a loyal following and a reputation for passenger consideration.

Southwest began to climb its way up. By 1978, it was one of the country's most profitable airlines. In the early 2000s, when many airlines suffered major setbacks, some going into bankruptcy and even going out of business, Southwest not only survived but led the industry in profitability.

Herb Kelleher gives this advice to success-minded people:
- Stick to your *ideas*. Despite efforts of its giant competitors to keep Southwest from entering the business, a positive attitude kept them going during three years of court fights and no operating income
- Think of what the customers want and then give it to them.
- Overcome obstacles put in your path by taking positive steps to break them down—and even while the battle is being fought, find ways to get around them.

- Keep open to new opportunities and, when they arise, take positive steps to meet them.

## More examples of imagination at work

Here are a few additional examples of the imaginative faculty at work:

- A publisher of books learned that many people buy titles and not contents of books. By merely changing the title of one book that was not selling, his sales on that book jumped upward more than a million copies. He merely ripped off the cover bearing the title that did not sell and put on a new cover with a more appealing title. That, as simple as it may seem, was an *idea*, the product of the *imagination*.
- The moving picture industry created a whole flock of millionaires. Most of them were men who couldn't create ideas, *but* they had the imagination to recognize ideas when they saw them.
- Andrew Carnegie knew very little about making steel—I have Carnegie's own word on this—but he had an idea and a plan and knew how to obtain the specialized knowledge required to execute it. Carnegie surrounded himself with experts who could do all that he could not do, people who created ideas and those who put ideas into operation, and made himself and the others fabulously rich.

The sixth sense is the door
to the Temple of Wisdom.

People become what they are
because of their *dominating
thoughts and desires.*

# Step 10

# Develop Your Sixth Sense

The *sixth sense* is a function of the creative imagination, the faculty of the subconscious mind through which Infinite Intelligence communicates voluntarily, without any effort from or demands by the individual. Although the sixth sense defies description and can be understood fully only by experiencing it, through meditation and mind development, you can begin to understand it through the roles it plays:

- Through the aid of the sixth sense, you are warned of impending dangers in time to avoid them and notified of opportunities in time to embrace them.
- The sixth sense probably is the medium of contact between the finite mind of individuals and Infinite Intelligence, and for this reason, it is a mixture of both the mental and the spiritual. It is believed to be the point at which the mind of an individual contacts the Universal Mind.

- There comes to your aid, and to do your bidding, with the development of the sixth sense, a "guardian angel" who will open to you at all times the door to the Temple of Wisdom.

You can profit by reading this book without understanding the principle described in this chapter, especially if your major purpose is that of accumulating money or other material things. This chapter on the sixth sense was included, because the book is designed to present a complete philosophy by which individuals may unerringly guide themselves in attaining whatever they ask of life. The starting point of all achievement is *desire*. The finishing point is that brand of *knowledge* that leads to understanding—understanding of self, understanding of others, understanding of the laws of Nature, recognition and understanding of *happiness*.

This sort of understanding comes in its fullness only through familiarity with and use of the principle of the sixth sense, hence that principle had to be included as a part of this philosophy, for the benefit of those who desire more than money.

Step by step, through the preceding chapters, you have been led to this, the last principle. If you have mastered each of the preceding principles, you are now prepared to accept, without being skeptical, the claims made here. If you have not mastered the other principles, you must do so before you may determine, definitely, whether or not the claims made in this chapter are fact or fiction.

## No believer in miracles

The author does not believe in miracles, because he has enough knowledge of Nature to understand that Nature never deviates from her established laws. Some of her laws are so incomprehensible that they produce what appear to be miracles. The sixth sense appears to be the tool that enables human beings to channel Infinite Intelligence to produce what are often referred to as "miracles"—events that seem to defy the laws of Nature only because we have no understanding of the method by which the sixth sense operates.

This much the author does know:

- There is a power or a First Cause or an Intelligence that permeates every atom of matter and embraces every unit of perceptible energy.
- This Infinite Intelligence converts acorns into oak trees, causes water to flow downhill in response to the law of gravity, and follows night with day and winter with summer, each maintaining its proper place and relationship to the other.
- Infinite Intelligence may, through the principles of this philosophy, be induced to aid in transmuting *desires* into concrete or material form.

The author has this knowledge, because he has experimented with it and has *experienced it.*

---

*Infinite Intelligence may, through the principles of this philosophy, be induced to aid in transmuting* desires *into concrete or material form.*

---

## My Invisible Counselors

While I was passing through the age of hero-worship, I found myself trying to imitate those whom I most admired. Moreover, I discovered that the element of faith, with which I endeavored to imitate my idols, gave me great capacity to do so quite successfully.

I have never entirely divested myself of this habit of hero-worship, although I have passed the age commonly given over to such. My experience has taught me that the next best thing to being truly great is to emulate the great, by feeling and action, as nearly as possible.

Long before I had ever written a line for publication or endeavored to deliver a speech in public, I followed the habit of reshaping my own character by trying to imitate the nine people whose lives and life-works had been most impressive to me: Emerson, Paine, Edison, Darwin, Lincoln, Burbank, Napoleon, Ford, and Carnegie. Every night, over a long period of years, I held an imaginary Council meeting with this group whom I called my "Invisible Counselors."

The procedure was this: Just before going to sleep at night, I would shut my eyes, and see, in my imagination, this group of men seated with me around my Council Table. Here I had not only an opportunity to sit among those whom I considered to be great, but I actually dominated the group by serving as the Chairman.

I had a very *definite purpose* in indulging my imagination through these nightly meetings. My purpose was to rebuild my own character so it would represent a composite of the characters of my imaginary counselors. Realizing, as I did early in life, that I had to overcome the handicap of birth in an environment of ignorance and superstition, I deliberately assigned myself the task of voluntary rebirth through the method here described.

## Building character through my Invisible Counselors

Being an earnest student of psychology, I knew, of course, that all people have become what they are because of their *dominating thoughts and desires*. I knew that every deeply seated desire has the effect of causing one to seek outward expression through which that desire may be transmuted into reality. I knew that self-suggestion is a powerful factor in building character, that it is, in fact, the sole principle through which character is built.

---

> People become what they are because of their *dominating thoughts and desires*.

---

With this knowledge of the principles of mind operation, I was fairly well armed with the equipment needed to rebuild my character. In these imaginary Council meetings I called on my Cabinet members for the knowledge I wished each to contribute, addressing myself to each member in audible words, as follows:

Mr. Emerson, I desire to acquire from you the marvelous understanding of Nature which distinguished your life. I ask that you make an impress upon my subconscious mind of whatever qualities you possessed that enabled you to understand and adapt yourself to the laws of Nature. I ask that you assist me in reaching and drawing upon whatever sources of knowledge are available to this end.

Mr. Burbank, I request that you pass on to me the knowledge that enabled you to so harmonize the laws of Nature that you caused the cactus to shed its thorns and become an edible food. Give me access to the knowledge that enabled you to make two blades of grass grow where but one grew before and helped you to blend the coloring of the flowers with more splendor and harmony, for you, alone, have successfully gilded the lily.

Mr. Napoleon, I desire to acquire from you, by emulation, the marvelous ability you possessed to inspire people and to arouse them to greater and more determined spirit of action. Also to acquire the spirit of enduring *faith* that enabled you to turn defeat into victory and to surmount staggering obstacles. Emperor of Fate, King of Chance, Man of Destiny, I salute you!

Mr. Paine, I desire to acquire from you the freedom of thought and the courage and clarity with which to express convictions, which so distinguished you!

Mr. Darwin, I wish to acquire from you the marvelous patience and ability to study cause and effect, without bias or prejudice, so exemplified by you in the field of natural science.

Mr. Lincoln, I desire to build into my own character the keen sense of justice, the untiring spirit of patience, the sense of humor, the human understanding, and the tolerance, which were your distinguishing characteristics.

Mr. Carnegie, I am already indebted to you for my choice of a life-work, which has brought me great happiness and peace of mind. I wish to acquire a thorough understanding of the principles of organized effort, which you used so effectively in the building of a great industrial enterprise.

Mr. Ford, you have been among the most helpful of the men who have supplied much of the material essential to my work.

I wish to acquire your spirit of persistence, the determination, poise, and self-confidence that have enabled you to master poverty, organize, unify, and simplify human effort, so I may help others to follow in your footsteps.

Mr. Edison, I have seated you nearest to me, at my right, because of the personal cooperation you have given me, during my research into the causes of success and failure. I wish to acquire from you the marvelous spirit of *faith*, with which you have uncovered so many of Nature's secrets, the spirit of unremitting toil with which you have so often wrested victory from defeat.

My method of addressing the members of the imaginary Cabinet would vary, according to the traits of character in which I was, for the moment, most interested in acquiring. I studied the records of their lives with painstaking care. After some months of this nightly procedure, I was astounded by the discovery that these imaginary figures became, apparently real.

Each of these nine men developed individual characteristics that surprised me. For example Lincoln developed the habit of always being late then walking around in solemn parade. When he came, he walked very slowly, with his hands clasped behind him, and once in a while, he would stop as he passed and rest his hand, momentarily, upon my shoulder. He always had a serious expression. Rarely did I see him smile. The cares of a sundered nation made him grave.

That was not true of the others. Burbank and Paine often indulged in witty repartee that seemed, at times, to shock the other members of the cabinet. One night Paine suggested that I prepare a lecture on "The Age of Reason" and deliver it from the pulpit of a church that I formerly attended. Many around the table laughed heartily at the suggestion. Not Napoleon! He drew his mouth down at the corners and groaned so loudly that all turned and looked at him with amazement. To him the church was but a pawn of the State, not to be reformed but to be used as a convenient inciter to mass activity by the people.

On one occasion, Burbank was late. When he came, he was excited with enthusiasm and explained that he had been late because of an experiment he was performing, through which he hoped to be able to grow apples on any sort of tree. Paine chided him by reminding him that it was an apple that started all the trouble between man and woman. Darwin chuckled heartily as he suggested that Paine should watch out for little serpents, when he went into the forest to gather apples, as they had the habit of growing into big snakes. Emerson observed, "No serpents, no apples," and Napoleon remarked, "No apples, no state!"

Lincoln developed the habit of always being the last one to leave the table after each meeting. On one occasion, he leaned across the end of the table, his arms folded, and remained in that position for many minutes. I made no attempt to disturb him. Finally, he lifted his head slowly, got up and walked to the door, then turned around, came back, and laid his hand on my shoulder and said, "My boy, you will need much courage if you remain steadfast in carrying out your purpose in life. But remember, when difficulties overtake you, the common people have common sense. Adversity will develop it."

One evening, Edison arrived ahead of all the others. He walked over and seated himself at my left, where Emerson was accustomed to sit, and said:

You are destined to witness the discovery of the secret of life. When the time comes, you will observe that life consists of great swarms of energy or entities, each as intelligent as human beings think themselves to be. These units of life group together like hives of bees, and remain together until they disintegrate, through lack of harmony.

These units have differences of opinion, the same as human beings, and often fight among themselves. These meetings you are conducting will be very helpful to you. They will bring to your rescue some of the same units of life that served the members of your Cabinet during their lives. These units are eternal. *They never die!* Your own thoughts and *desires* serve as the magnet that attracts units of life from the great ocean of life out there. Only the friendly units are attracted—the ones that harmonize with the nature of your *desires*.

The other members of the Cabinet began to enter the room. Edison got up, and slowly walked around to his own seat. Edison was still living when this happened. It impressed me so greatly that I went to see him and told him about the experience. He smiled broadly, and said, "Your dream was more a reality than you may imagine it to have been." He added no further explanation to his statement.

These meetings became so realistic that I became fearful of their consequences and discontinued them for several months. The experiences were so uncanny, I was afraid if I continued them I would lose sight of the fact that the meetings were purely experiences of my imagination.

Six months after I had discontinued the practice I was awakened one night, or thought I was, when I saw Lincoln standing at my bedside. He said, "The world will soon need your services. It is about to undergo a period of chaos that will cause men and women to lose faith and become panic stricken.

Go ahead with your work and complete your philosophy. That is your mission in life. If you neglect it, for any cause whatsoever, you will be reduced to a primal state, and be compelled to retrace the cycles through which you have passed during thousands of years."

I was unable to tell, the following morning, whether I had dreamed this or had actually been awake, and I have never since found out which it was, but I do know that the dream, if it were a dream, was so vivid in my mind the next day that I resumed my meetings the following night.

At our next meeting, the members of my Cabinet all filed into the room together and stood at their accustomed places at the Council Table, while Lincoln raised a glass and said, "Gentlemen, let us drink a toast to a friend who has returned to the fold."

After that, I began to add new members to my Cabinet, until now it consists of more than fifty, among them Christ, St. Paul, Galileo, Copernicus, Aristotle, Plato, Socrates, Homer, Voltaire, Bruno, Spinoza, Drummond, Kant, Schopenhauer, Newton, Confucius, Elbert Hubbard, Brann, Ingersol, Wilson, and William James.

This is the first time that I have had the courage to mention this. Heretofore, I have remained quiet on the subject, because I knew, from my own attitude in connection with such matters, that I would be misunderstood if I described my unusual experience. I have been emboldened now to reduce my experience to the printed page, because I am now less concerned about what "they say" than I was in the years that have passed. One of the blessings of maturity is that it sometimes brings one greater courage to be truthful, regardless of what those who do not understand may think or say.

## Receiving knowledge and guidance through the sixth sense

Lest I be misunderstood, I wish here to state most emphatically that I still regard my Cabinet meetings as being purely imaginary, but while the members of my Cabinet may be purely fictional, and the meetings existent only in my own imagination, they have led me into glorious paths of adventure, rekindled an appreciation of true greatness, encouraged creative endeavor, and emboldened the expression of honest thought.

During meetings with my Invisible Counselors, I find my mind most receptive to ideas, thoughts, and knowledge that reach me through the sixth sense. I can truthfully say that I owe entirely to my Invisible Counselors full credit for such ideas, facts, and knowledge as I received through inspiration.

Somewhere in the cell structure of the brain is located an organ that receives vibrations of thought ordinarily called "hunches." So far, science has not discovered where this organ of the sixth sense is located, but this is not important. The fact remains that human beings do receive accurate knowledge through sources other than the physical senses. Such knowledge, generally, is received when the mind is under the influence of extraordinary stimulation. Any emergency that arouses the emotions and causes the heart to beat more rapidly than normal may, and generally does, bring the sixth sense into action. Anyone who has experienced a near accident while driving knows that on such occasions, the sixth sense often comes to one's rescue and aids, by split seconds, in avoiding the accident.

On scores of occasions, when I have faced emergencies, some of them so grave that my life was in jeopardy, I have been miraculously guided past these difficulties through the influence of my Invisible Counselors.

---

Any emergency that arouses the emotions
brings the sixth sense into action.

---

My original purpose in conducting Council meetings with imaginary beings was solely that of impressing my own subconscious mind, through the principle of autosuggestion, with certain characteristics that I desired to acquire. In more recent years, my experimentation has taken on an entirely different trend. I now go to my imaginary counselors with every difficult problem that confronts my clients and me. The results are often astonishing, although I do not depend entirely on this form of counsel.

## Great leaders and the sixth sense

Nearly all great leaders, including Napoleon, Joan of Arc, Christ, Buddha, Confucius, and Mohammed understood and probably made use of the sixth sense almost continuously. The major portion of their greatness consisted of their knowledge of this principle.

Henry Ford undoubtedly understood and made practical use of the sixth sense. His vast business and financial operations made it necessary for him to understand and use this principle. Thomas A. Edison understood and used the sixth sense in connection with the development of inventions, especially those involving basic patents in connection with which he had no human experience and no accumulated knowledge to guide him, as was the case while he was working on the talking machine and the moving picture machine.

The sixth sense is not something that one can take off and put on at will. Ability to use this great power comes slowly, through application of the other principles outlined in this book. Seldom does any individual come into workable knowledge of the sixth sense before the age of forty. More often the knowledge is not available until one is well past fifty, because the spiritual forces, with which the sixth sense is so closely related, do not mature and become usable except through years of meditation, self-examination, and serious thought.

Having read the chapter, you must have observed that while reading it, you were lifted to a high level of mental stimulation. Splendid! Come back to this again a month from now, read it once more, and observe that your mind will soar to a still higher level of stimulation. Repeat this experience from time to time, giving no concern as to how much or how little you learn at the time, and eventually you will find yourself in possession of a power that will enable you to throw off discouragement, master fear, overcome procrastination, and draw freely upon your imagination. Then you will have felt the touch of that unknown "something" which has been the moving spirit of every truly great thinker leader, artist, musician, writer, and statesperson. Then you will be in position to transmute your *desires* into their physical or financial counterpart as easily as you may lie down and quit at the first sign of opposition.

*Sex transmutation* is the switching of the mind from thoughts of physical sexual expression to thoughts of some other nature.

The transmutation of sexual desire drives the creative imagination.

Sex transmutation will lift one to the status of a genius.

# Step 11

# Crack the Mystery of Sex Transmutation

In simple language, *transmutation* is the conversion of one element or form of energy into another. *Sex transmutation* is the switching of the mind from thoughts of physical sexual expression to thoughts of some other nature.

Sexual desire brings into being a state of mind that is generally associated with the physical but holds the possibility of the following three constructive potentialities:

- The perpetuation of mankind
- The maintenance of health (As a therapeutic agency, it has no equal.)
- The transformation of mediocrity into genius through transmutation

Sexual desire is the most powerful of human desires. When driven by this desire, people develop keenness of imagination, courage, willpower, persistence, and creative ability unknown to them at other times. So strong and impelling is the desire for sexual contact that people freely run the risk of life and reputation to indulge it. When harnessed and redirected along other lines, this motivating force maintains all of its attributes of keenness of imagination, courage, etc., which may be used as powerful creative forces in literature, art, or in any other profession or calling, including, of course, the accumulation of riches.

The transmutation of sexual energy calls for the exercise of willpower, to be sure, but the reward is worth the effort. The desire for sexual expression is inborn and natural. The desire cannot and should not be repressed or eliminated. Instead, it should be given an outlet through forms of expression that enrich the body, mind, and spirit. If not given this form of outlet, through transmutation, it will seek outlets through purely physical channels.

---

> A river may be dammed and its water controlled for a time, but eventually it will force an outlet. The same is true of sexual energy. It may be repressed and controlled for a time, but its very nature causes it to continuously seek means of expression. If it is not transmuted into some creative effort it will find a less worthy outlet.

---

Sexual desire is an irresistible force against which there can be no such opposition as an immovable body. When driven by this emotion, people become gifted with a super power for action. *Sex transmutation can lift one to the status of genius.* A *genius* is a person who has discovered how to increase the vibrations of thought to the point at which he or she can freely communicate with sources of knowledge unavailable through the ordinary rate of vibration of thought—knowledge stored in one's own subconscious, in the subconscious minds of others, and *Infinite Intelligence*.

---

> The world is ruled, and the destiny of civilization is established, by the human emotions. People are stirred to action not by reason so much as by feelings. The creative faculty of the mind is set into action entirely by emotions and not by cold reason. The most powerful of all human emotions is that of sex.

---

## The ten mind stimulants

The human mind responds to stimuli. A *mind stimulant* is any influence that temporarily or permanently increases the vibrations of thought known as enthusiasm, creative imagination, intense desire, etc. Through these sources, one may commune with Infinite Intelligence or enter, at will, the storehouse of the subconscious mind, either one's own or that of another person, thus achieving a state of *genius*. The stimuli to which the mind responds most freely are:

1. Sexual desire
2. Love
3. A burning desire for fame, power, or financial gain, *money*
4. Music
5. Friendship with those of the same or opposite sex
6. A *Master Mind alliance* based upon the harmony of two or more people who ally themselves for spiritual or temporal advancement

7. Mutual suffering, such as that experienced by people who are persecuted
8. Autosuggestion
9. Fear
10. Artificial mind stimulants, such as narcotics and alcohol

Note that this is not a comprehensive list of mind stimulants; these are only the ten stimuli to which the mind responds most freely. And not one of them, nor all of them combined, equals the driving power of sex. (Note also that the first eight of these stimuli are constructive, whereas the final two are, or at least can be, destructive.)

---

Sexual desire is, by far, the most intense and powerful of all mind stimuli, far more potent than all of the others combined.

---

## How to transmute sex

The road to genius consists of the *development, control, and use* of sexual energy, so it follows that transmutation of sex is a cyclical three-step process:

1. **Development:** Encourage the presence of sex, love, and romance as the dominating thoughts in your mind, and discourage the presence of all the destructive emotions (such as fear and jealousy). For more about the benefits of combining sex with love and romance, see the later section, "Combining sex, love, and romance."

    The mind is a creature of habit. It thrives upon the dominating thoughts fed it. Through the faculty of willpower, you may encourage or discourage the presence of

any emotion. When any negative emotion presents itself in your mind, it can be transmuted into a positive, constructive emotion by the simple procedure of changing your thoughts.
2. **Control:** Resist the temptation to overindulge in physical forms of sexual expression. Allow the emotions of sex, love, and romance to intensify as you continue to nurture them.
3. **Use:** Quiet your rational mind by removing all distractions and focus on the financial object you desire, the goal you will ultimately achieve, the opportunity you are pursuing, the problem you must solve, or whatever creative endeavor you are immersed in. You may want to sit or lie down in a quiet, dark or dimly lit room or close your eyes to allow your subconscious mind to take over as your thought vibrations intensify.

*There is no other road to genius than through voluntary self-effort!* People may attain to great heights of financial or business achievement solely by the driving force of sex energy, but history is filled with evidence that they may, and usually do, carry with them certain character traits that rob them of the ability to either hold or enjoy their good fortune.

## Engaging the sixth sense through the transmutation of sex

The transmutation of sex engages the *sixth sense*—creative imagination, which is covered in more depth in Step 10. The faculty of creative imagination is one that the majority of people never use during an entire lifetime, and, if used at all, it is usually by mere accident. A relatively small number of people use the faculty of creative imagination *with deliberation and purposeful forethought*. Those who use this faculty voluntarily and with understanding of its functions are *geniuses*.

The faculty of creative imagination is the direct link between the finite mind of humans and Infinite Intelligence. All so-called revelations referred to in the realm of religion and all discoveries of basic or new principles in the field of invention take place through the faculty of creative imagination. When ideas or concepts flash into one's mind, through what is popularly called a "hunch," they come from one or more of the following sources:

- Infinite Intelligence
- One's subconscious mind, wherein is stored every sense impression and thought impulse that ever reached the brain through any of the five senses
- The mind of some other person who has just released the thought or picture of the idea or concept through conscious thought, or
- The other person's subconscious storehouse

There are no other *known* sources from which "inspired" ideas or "hunches" may be received.

### Reaching a higher thought plane

The creative imagination functions best when the mind is vibrating (due to some form of mind stimulation) at an exceedingly high rate; that is, when the mind is functioning at a rate of vibration higher than that of ordinary, normal thought.

When harnessed and transmuted, this driving force is capable of lifting one into that higher sphere of thought, which enables them to master the sources of worry and petty annoyance that beset their pathway on the lower plane. It lifts the individual far above the horizon of ordinary thought, allowing him or her to envision distance, scope, and quality of *thoughts* not available on the lower plane, such as that occupied while one is engaged in the solution of the problems of business and professional routine.

When lifted to this higher thought plane, an individual occupies relatively the same position as one who has ascended in an airplane to a height from which one may see over and beyond the horizon that limits one's vision while on the ground. Moreover, while on this higher thought plane, the individual is not hampered or bound by any of the stimuli that circumscribe and restrict his or her vision while wrestling with the problems of gaining the three basic necessities of food, clothing, and shelter. He or she is in a world of thought in which the *ordinary*, work-a-day thoughts have been as effectively removed as are the hills and valleys and other limitations of physical vision when rising in an airplane.

While on this exalted *thought* plane, the creative faculty of the mind is given freedom for action. The way has been cleared for the sixth sense to function; it becomes receptive to ideas that could not reach the individual under any other circumstances.

---

**The *sixth sense* is the faculty that marks the difference between a genius and an ordinary individual.**

---

The creative faculty becomes more alert and receptive to external vibrations the more it is used, and the more the individual relies upon it and makes demands upon it for thought impulses. This faculty can be cultivated and developed only through use.

Unfortunately, only the geniuses have made the discovery. Others have experienced sexual energy without discovering one of its major potentialities—a fact that accounts for the great number of "others" as compared to the limited number of geniuses.

### Reason versus creative imagination

The reasoning faculty is often faulty, because it is largely guided by one's accumulated experience. Not all knowledge, which one accumulates through "experience," is accurate. Ideas received through the creative faculty are much more reliable, because they come from sources more reliable than any which are available to the reasoning faculty of the mind.

The major difference between the genius and the ordinary "crank" inventor may be found in the fact that the genius works through his faculty of creative imagination, while the "crank" knows nothing of this faculty. The scientific inventor makes use of both the synthetic and the creative faculties of imagination.

For example, scientific inventors (geniuses) begin an invention by organizing and combining the known ideas, or principles accumulated through experience, through the synthetic faculty (the reasoning faculty). If they find this accumulated knowledge to be insufficient for completing the invention, they then draw upon the sources of knowledge available to them through their creative faculty. The method by which this is

done varies with the individual, but this is the sum and substance of the procedure:
1. *They stimulate their minds so that they vibrate on a higher-than-average plane*, using one or more of the ten mind stimulants or some other stimulant of his or her choice.
2. *They concentrate* upon the known factors (the finished part) of the invention and create in their minds a perfect picture of unknown factors (the unfinished part) of the invention. They hold this picture in mind until it has been taken over by the subconscious mind and then relax by clearing their minds of *all* thought and wait for the answer to pop up.

Sometimes the results are both definite and immediate. At other times, the results are negative, depending upon the state of development of the sixth sense, the creative faculty.

---

> Mr. Edison tried out more than 10,000 different combinations of ideas through the synthetic faculty of his imagination before he "tuned in" through the creative faculty, and got the answer that perfected the incandescent light. His experience was similar when he produced the talking machine.

---

## Dr. Elmer R. Gates: Cultivating and using the creative faculty

Dr. Elmer R. Gates, of Chevy Chase, Maryland, created more than 200 useful patents, many of them basic, through the process of cultivating and using the creative faculty. His method is both significant and interesting to one interested in attaining to the status of genius, in which category Dr. Gates unquestionably belonged. Dr. Gates was one of the really great, though less publicized, scientists of the world.

In his laboratory, he had what he called his "personal communication room." It was practically sound proof and so arranged that all light could be shut out. It was equipped with a small table, on which he kept a pad of writing paper. In front of the table, on the wall, was a button that controlled the lights. When Dr. Gates desired to draw upon the forces available to him through his creative imagination, he would go into this room, seat himself at the table, shut off the lights, and *concentrate* upon the *known* factors of the invention on which he was working, remaining in that position until ideas began to "flash" into his mind in connection with the *unknown* factors of the invention.

On one occasion, ideas came through so fast that he was forced to write for almost three hours. When the thoughts stopped flowing, and he examined his notes, he found they contained a minute description of principles without parallel among the known data of the scientific world. Moreover, the answer to his problem was intelligently presented in those notes. In this manner, Dr. Gates completed over 200 patents, which had been begun, but not completed, by "half-baked" brains. Evidence of the truth of this statement is in the United States Patent Office.

Dr. Gates earned his living by "sitting for ideas" for individuals and corporations. Some of the largest corporations in America paid him substantial fees, by the hour, to "sit for ideas."

### The creative imagination at work in other fields

The great artists, writers, musicians, and poets become great, because they acquire the habit of relying upon the "still small voice" that speaks from within, through the faculty of creative imagination. It is a fact well known to people who have "keen" imaginations that their best ideas come through so-called "hunches."

There is a great orator who does not attain to greatness until he closes his eyes and begins to rely entirely upon the faculty of creative imagination. When asked why he closed his eyes just before the climaxes of his oratory, he replied, "I do it, because then I speak through ideas which come to me from within."

One of America's most successful and best-known financiers followed the habit of closing his eyes for two or three minutes before making a decision. When asked why he did this, he replied, "With my eyes closed, I am able to draw upon a source of superior intelligence."

### Sex energy and personal magnetism

A teacher, who has trained and directed the efforts of more than 30,000 sales people, made the astounding discovery that highly sexed people are the most efficient sales reps. The explanation is that the factor of personality known as "personal magnetism" is nothing more nor less than sexual energy. Highly sexed people always have a plentiful supply of magnetism. Through cultivation and understanding, this vital force may be drawn upon and used to great advantage in the relationships between people. This energy may be communicated to others through the following media:

- **Handshake:** The touch of the hand indicates, instantly, the presence or lack of magnetism.
- **Tone of voice:** Magnetism, or sex energy, colors the voice or makes it musical and charming.
- **Posture and carriage of the body:** Highly sexed people move briskly with grace and ease.
- **Vibrations of thought:** Highly sexed people mix the emotion of sex with their thoughts, or may do so at will, and in that way may influence those around them.
- **Body adornment:** People who are highly sexed are usually very careful about their personal appearance. They usually select clothing of a style becoming to their personality, physique, complexion, etc.

When employing salespeople, the more capable sales manager looks for the quality of personal magnetism as the first requirement for the job. People who lack sex energy will never become enthusiastic nor inspire others with enthusiasm, and enthusiasm is one of the most important requisites in salesmanship, no matter what one is selling. The public speaker, orator, preacher, lawyer, or salesperson who is lacking in sex energy is a "flop," as far as being able to influence others is concerned.

Couple with this the fact, that most people can be influenced only through an appeal to their emotions, and you will understand the importance of sex energy as a part of the salesperson's native ability. Master sales reps attain the status of mastery in selling, because they, either consciously, or unconsciously, transmute the energy of sex into *sales enthusiasm!*

Sales people who know how to take their minds off the subject of sex and direct it in sales effort with as much enthusiasm and determination as they would apply to its original purpose, have acquired the art of sex transmutation, whether they know it or not.

---

> The majority of sales people who transmute their sex energy do so without being in the least aware of what they are doing, or how they are doing it.

---

Transmutation of sex energy calls for more willpower than the average person cares to use for this purpose. Those who find it difficult to summon willpower sufficient for transmutation may gradually acquire this ability. Though this requires willpower, the reward for the practice is more than worth the effort.

## Gaining a deeper understanding of sex

The entire subject of sex is one with which the majority of people appear to be unpardonably ignorant. Sexuality been grossly misunderstood, slandered, and burlesqued by the ignorant and the evil minded for so long that the very word "sex" is seldom used in polite society. Men and women who are known to be blessed—yes, *blessed*—with highly sexed natures, are usually considered to be people around whom one must be careful. Instead of being called blessed, they are usually considered cursed.

Millions of people, even in this age of enlightenment, have inferiority complexes that they developed because of this false belief that a highly sexed nature is a curse. These statements, regarding the virtue of sex energy, should not be construed as justification for the libertine. Sexual urge is a virtue *only* when used intelligently and discriminately. It may be misused, and often is, to such an extent that it debases, instead of enriches, both body and mind. Sex transmutation redirects this power to more productive endeavors.

> A highly sexed nature is a blessing, not a curse.

Widespread ignorance on the subject of sex is due to the fact that the subject has been surrounded with mystery and beclouded by dark silence. The conspiracy of mystery and silence has increased curiosity and desire to acquire more knowledge on this "verboten" subject. To the shame of all lawmakers and most physicians—by training, those best qualified to educate youth on that subject—such information has not been easily available.

## Combining sex, love, and romance

Sex alone is a mighty urge to action, but its forces are like a cyclone—they are often uncontrollable. When the emotion of love begins to mix itself with the emotion of sex, the result is calmness of purpose, poise, accuracy of judgment, and balance.

Sex, love, and romance are all emotions capable of driving people to heights of super achievement. Love is a modulator that ensures balance, poise, and constructive effort. When combined, these three emotions may lift one to an altitude of a genius. Some geniuses, however, have little or no love. Most of them may be found engaged in some form of action which is destructive or not based upon justice and fairness toward others. If good taste would permit, a dozen geniuses could be named in the field of industry and finance who ride ruthlessly over the rights of others. They seem totally lacking in conscience.

---

> When combined, the emotions of sex, love, and romance may lift one to an altitude of a genius.

---

### Love softens, modifies, and beautifies

The emotions of love and sex leave their unmistakable marks upon the features. Moreover, these signs are so visible, that all who wish may read them. People who are driven by the storm of passion, based upon sex desires alone, plainly advertise that fact to the entire world by the expression of their eyes and the lines of their faces. The emotion of love, when mixed with the emotion of sex, softens, modifies, and beautifies the facial expression. No character analyst is needed to tell you this. You may observe it for yourself.

The emotion of love brings out, and develops, the artistic and the aesthetic nature of a person. It leaves its impress upon one's very soul, even after the fire has been subdued by time and circumstance.

Memories of love never pass. They linger, guide, and influence long after the source of stimulation has faded. There is nothing new in this. Every person who has been moved by *genuine love* knows that it leaves enduring traces upon the human heart. The effect of love endures, because love is spiritual in nature. Those who cannot be stimulated to great heights of achievement by love are hopeless—they are dead, though they may seem to live.

Even the memories of love are sufficient to lift one to a higher plane of creative effort. The major force of love may spend itself and pass away like a fire that has burned itself out, but it leaves behind indelible marks as evidence that it passed that way. Its departure often prepares the human heart for a still greater love.

Go back into your yesterdays and bathe your mind in the beautiful memories of past love. It will soften the influence of any present worries and annoyances. It will give you a source of escape from the unpleasant realities of life, and maybe —who knows?—your mind will yield to you, during this temporary retreat into the world of fantasy, ideas or plans that may change the entire financial or spiritual status of your life.

If you believe yourself unfortunate, because you have "loved and lost," perish the thought. One who has loved truly can never lose entirely. Love is whimsical and temperamental. Its nature is ephemeral and transitory. It comes when it pleases and goes away without warning. Accept and enjoy it while it remains, but spend no time worrying about its departure. Worry will never bring it back.

Dismiss, also, the thought that love never comes but once. Love may come and go countless times, but there are no two love experiences that affect one in just the same way. There may be, and there usually is, one love experience that leaves a deeper imprint on the heart than all the others, but all love experiences are beneficial, except to the person who becomes resentful and cynical when love makes its departure.

There should be no disappointment over love, and there would be none if people understood the difference between the emotions of love and sex. The major difference is that love is spiritual, while sex is biological. No experience that touches the human heart with a spiritual force can possibly be harmful, except through ignorance or jealousy.

---

> The main difference between love and sex is that love is spiritual, whereas sex is biological.

---

Love is, without question, life's greatest experience. It brings one into communion with Infinite Intelligence. When mixed with the emotions of romance and sex, it may lead one far up the ladder of creative effort. The emotions of love, sex, and romance, are sides of the eternal triangle of achievement-building genius. Nature creates geniuses through no other force.

## Linking sex to success

Scientific research on the backgrounds of high achieving men (unfortunately, no similar studies have been made about highly successful women) has disclosed these significant facts:

- The men of greatest achievement are men with highly developed sex natures; men who have learned the art of sex transmutation. Sex energy is the creative energy of all geniuses. There never has been, and never will be a great leader, builder, or artist lacking in this driving force of sex.
- The men who have accumulated great fortunes and achieved outstanding recognition in literature, art, industry, architecture, and the professions were motivated by the influence of a woman.

Surely no one will misunderstand these statements to mean that *all* who are highly sexed are geniuses! One attains to the status of a genius *only* when, and *if,* one's mind is stimulated so that it draws upon the forces available, through the creative faculty of the imagination. The mere possession of sexual energy is not sufficient to produce a genius. The energy must be transmuted from desire for physical contact into some other form of desire and action, before it will lift one to the status of a genius.

### A destructive combination

Emotions (including sex, love, and romance) are states of mind. Nature has provided us with a "chemistry of the mind" that operates in a manner similar to the principles of chemistry of matter. It is a well-known fact that, through the aid of chemistry of matter, a chemist may create a deadly poison by mixing certain elements, none of which are—in themselves—harmful in the right proportions. Likewise, the emotions may be combined so as to create a deadly poison. For example, the emotions of sex and jealousy, when mixed, may turn a person into an insane beast.

The presence of any one or more of the destructive emotions in the human mind, through the chemistry of the mind, sets up a poison that may destroy one's sense of justice and fairness. In extreme cases, the presence of any combination of these emotions in the mind may destroy one's reason.

## The use of artificial mind stimulants

History is not lacking in examples of people who attained to the status of geniuses as the result of the use of artificial mind stimulants in the form of alcohol and narcotics:

- Edgar Allen Poe wrote "The Raven" while under the influence of liquor, "dreaming dreams that mortal never dared to dream before."
- James Whitcomb Riley did his best writing while under the influence of alcohol. Perhaps it was thus he saw "the ordered intermingling of the real and the dream, the mill above the river, and the mist above the stream."
- Robert Burns wrote best when intoxicated, "For Auld Lang Syne, my dear, we'll take a cup of kindness yet, for Auld Lang Syne."

**Remember:** Many such people have destroyed themselves in the end. Nature has prepared her own potions with which people may safely stimulate their minds so they vibrate on a plane that enables them to tune in to fine and rare thoughts that come from "the great unknown!" No satisfactory substitute for Nature's stimulants has ever been found.

## Why people seldom succeed before 40

Based on my analysis of over 25,000 people, people who succeed in an outstanding way seldom do so before the age of 40, and more often they do not strike their real pace until they are well beyond the age of 50. The greatest capacity to create for the average person is between 40 and 60. This fact was so astounding that it prompted me to go into the study of its cause most carefully, carrying the investigation over a period of more than twelve years.

This study disclosed the fact that the major reason why the majority of people who succeed do not begin to do so before the age of 40 to 50 is their tendency to *dissipate* their energies through overindulgence in physical expression of sex. Most people never learn that sexual urge has other possibilities that transcend in importance that of mere physical expression. The majority of those who make this discovery do so after wasting many years when the sex energy is at its height, prior to the age of 45 to 50. This usually is followed by noteworthy achievement.

Biographies of American industrialists and financiers are filled with evidence that the period from 40 to 60 is the most productive age. Here are three examples:

- Henry Ford had not "hit his pace" of achievement until he had passed the age of 40.
- Andrew Carnegie was well past 40 before he began to reap the reward of his efforts.
- James J. Hill was still running a telegraph key at the age of 40. His stupendous achievements took place after that age.

The lives of many people up to and sometimes well past the age of 40 reflect a continued dissipation of energies, which could have been more profitably turned into better channels. Their finer and more powerful emotions are sown wildly to the four winds. Out of this habit grew the term, "sowing one's wild oats."

Between the ages of 30 and 40, one begins to learn (if one ever learns), the art of sex transmutation. This discovery is generally accidental, and more often than otherwise, the persons who make it are totally unconscious of this discovery. They may observe that their powers of achievement have increased around the age of 35 to 40, but in most cases, they are not familiar with the cause of this change: Nature begins to harmonize the emotions of love and sex in the individual, between the ages of 30 and 40, so that they may draw upon these great forces and apply them jointly as stimuli to action.

---

> This should be encouraging to those who fail to arrive before the age of 40 and to those who become frightened at the approach of "old age," around the 40-year mark. One should approach this age, not with fear and trembling, but with hope and eager anticipation.

---

## Overindulgence in sex

Intemperance in sex habits is just as detrimental as intemperance in habits of drinking and eating. In this age in which we live, an age that began with the First World War, intemperance in habits of sex is common. This orgy of indulgence may account for the shortage of great leaders. No one can avail the forces of creative imagination while dissipating them. Humans are the only creatures on earth that violate Nature's purpose in this connection. Every other animal indulges its sex nature in moderation and with purpose that harmonizes with the laws of nature. Every other animal responds to the call of sex only in "season." The human inclination is to declare "open season."

Every intelligent person knows that stimulation in excess, through alcoholic drink and narcotics, is a form of intemperance that destroys the vital organs of the body, including the brain. Not every person knows, however, that overindulgence in sexual desire may become a habit as destructive and as detrimental to creative effort as narcotics or liquor.

> Far from becoming geniuses because of great sex desires, all too many people lower themselves, through misunderstanding and misuse of this great force, to the status of the lower animals.

A sex-mad person is not essentially different than a dope-mad person! Both have lost control over their faculties of reason and willpower. Overindulgence in sexual desire may not only destroy reason and willpower, but it may also lead to either temporary or permanent insanity. Many cases of hypochondria (imaginary illness) grow out of habits developed in ignorance of the true function of sex.

From these brief references to the subject, it may be readily seen that ignorance on the subject of sex transmutation, forces stupendous penalties upon the ignorant on the one hand, and withholds from them equally stupendous benefits, on the other.

The human brain is a broadcasting and receiving station for thought.

Thought vibration, stepped up by emotion, can be broadcast and received by the brain.

Your intangible (unseen) self is more powerful than the physical self you perceive.

# Step 12

# Empower Your Brain: Mental Telepathy and Clairvoyance

In a study by the author with Dr. Alexander Graham Bell and Dr. Elmer R. Gates, it was concluded that every human brain is both a broadcasting and receiving station for the vibration of thought.

Through the medium of the ether, in a fashion similar to that employed by the basic principle of radio and other wireless communication, every human brain is capable of picking up vibrations of thought released by other brains and those present in Infinite Intelligence. Hence, the human brain is capable of mental telepathy and clairvoyance.

- **Mental telepathy** is the process of transferring thoughts directly from one brain to another without sensory means of communication.

- **Clairvoyance** (or extrasensory perception) is the faculty of obtaining information about a person, place, thing, or event without physically observing, experiencing, or hearing about it.

## How the mental broadcasting system works

The mental broadcasting system involves the subconscious mind, creative imagination, and autosuggestion.

### The subconscious mind

The subconscious mind (see Step 6) is the "antenna" through which high-intensity thought vibrations pass. It is the conduit of communication between the conscious, reasoning mind and the four sources from which one may receive thought stimuli: Infinite intelligence, your own subconscious mind, another person's conscious thought, or another person's subconscious thought. (For more about these four sources, see Step 11 on sex transmutation.)

Thought vibrations of an exceedingly high rate travel through the ether from one brain to another. Thought that has been stepped up by any of the major emotions vibrates at a much higher rate than ordinary thought, and it is this energized thought that passes from one brain to another, via the broadcasting machinery of the human brain.

---

*Thought vibrations, stepped up by emotion, travel through the either from one brain to another.*

---

## Creative imagination

Creative imagination (covered in Step 9) is like the tuning mechanism on a radio. When a thought mixed with emotion reaches a high rate of vibration in the mind, the creative imagination "tunes in" to that thought and related thoughts that reach it through the ether from outside sources and from the subconscious.

---

**Remember:** Both positive and negative emotions (see Step 11) can step up a thought to a high rate of vibration. You must be careful to stimulate a thought only with positive emotions to ensure a positive outcome.

---

The positive emotion of sex stands at the head of the list of human emotions in terms of intensity and driving force. Stimulated by the emotion of sex, thoughts vibrate at a much more rapid rate than they do when that emotion is quiescent or absent.

The result of sex transmutation is the increase of the rate of vibration of thoughts to such a pitch that the creative imagination becomes highly receptive to ideas from the four sources of thought stimuli.

## Autosuggestion

Stepped up vibration not only attracts thoughts and ideas released by other brains through the medium of the ether, but it gives to one's own thoughts the emotion required for those thoughts to be impressed upon and acted upon by one's subconscious mind. For example, by mixing desire with the emotion of faith and passing it along to your subconscious mind via autosuggestion, you impress upon your subconscious that you *will* receive that which you desire.

This stepped up thought (desire mixed with emotion) is also conveyed to your creative imagination and broadcast out into the ether, where it becomes a part of Infinite Intelligence and can be picked up by other brains. Your creative imagination can then begin to develop a plan by which you will receive that which you desire, drawing from all four sources of thought stimuli to create such a plan. (For more about using autosuggestion to impress desire on your subconscious mind, turn to Step 6.)

---

Autosuggestion is the means by which thought mixed with emotion is impressed upon the subconscious mind.

---

## The greatest forces are intangible

Through the ages that have passed, people have depended too much upon their physical senses and have limited their knowledge to physical things that can be seen, touched, weighed, and measured. The Great Depression of the 1930s brought the world to the very borderline of understanding the power of intangible, unseen forces. Nothing in the physical world had changed, but overconfidence in the U.S. stock market followed by a complete lack of confidence in the economy brought the United States and many other industrialized countries to their knees.

We are now entering the most marvelous of all ages—an age that will teach us something of the intangible forces of the world around us. Perhaps we shall learn, as we pass through this age, that the "other self" is more powerful than the physical self we see when you look in a mirror.

> Your "other self," your intangible self, is more powerful than the physical self you see when you look in a mirror.

Sometimes we speak lightly of the intangibles—the things that we cannot perceive through any of our five senses—but we should never forget that all of us are controlled by forces that are unseen and intangible.

The whole of humankind has not the power to cope with, nor to control the intangible force wrapped up in the rolling waves of the oceans. The human mind does not have the capacity to understand the intangible force of gravity, which keeps this little earth suspended in mid-air, and keeps us from falling from it, much less the power to control that force. All of us are entirely subservient to the intangible force which comes with a thunder storm, and we are just as helpless in the presence of the intangible force of electricity. Indeed, many of us do not even know what electricity is, where it comes from, or what is its purpose!

Nor is this by any means the end of our ignorance in connection with things unseen and intangible. We do not understand the intangible force (and intelligence) wrapped up in the soil of the earth—the force that provides us with every morsel of food we eat, every article of clothing we wear, every dollar we carry in our pockets.

## The dramatic story of the brain

With all of our boasted culture and education, we understand little or nothing of the intangible force (the greatest of all the intangibles) of thought. We know but little concerning the physical brain and its vast network of intricate machinery through which the power of thought is translated into its material equivalent, but we are now entering an age that shall yield enlightenment on the subject. Already scientists have begun to turn their attention to the study of this stupendous thing called a brain, and, while they are still in the kindergarten stage of their studies, they have uncovered enough knowledge to know that the central switchboard of the human brain comprises nearly 200 billion neurons and at least several hundred trillion connections!

"The figure is so stupendous," said Dr. C. Judson Herrick, of the University of Chicago, "that astronomical figures dealing with hundreds of millions of light years, become insignificant by comparison." Herrick also points out that the nerve cells in the cerebral cortex are arranged in definite patterns, "These arrangements are not haphazard. They are orderly. Recently developed methods of electro-physiology draw off action currents from very precisely located cells, or fibers with micro-electrodes, amplify them, and record potential differences to a millionth of a volt."

It is inconceivable that such a network of intricate machinery should be in existence for the sole purpose of carrying on the physical functions incidental to growth and maintenance of the physical body. Is it unlikely that the same system, which gives billions of brain cells the media for communication one with another, also provides the means of communication with other intangible forces?

> It is inconceivable that such a network of intricate machinery should exist for the sole purpose of carrying on the physical functions incidental to growth and maintenance of the physical body.

In the late 1930s, *The New York Times* published an editorial showing that at least one great University, and one intelligent investigator in the field of mental phenomena, were carrying on an organized research through which conclusions had been reached that parallel many of those described in this and the following step. The editorial briefly analyzed the work carried on by Dr. Rhine, and his associates at Duke University:

## What is "Telepathy"?

A month ago we cited on this page some of the remarkable results achieved by Professor Rhine and his associates in Duke University from more than a hundred thousand tests to determine the existence of "telepathy" and "clairvoyance." These results were summarized in the first two articles in *Harper's Magazine*. In the second that has now appeared, the author, E. H. Wright, attempts to summarize what has been learned, or what it seems reasonable to infer, regarding the exact nature of these "extrasensory" modes of perception:

The actual existence of telepathy and clairvoyance now seems to some scientists enormously probable as the result of Rhine's experiments. Various percipients were asked to name as many cards in a special pack as they could without looking at them and without other sensory access to them. About a score of men and women were discovered who could regularly name so many of the cards correctly that "there was not one chance in many a million of their having done their feats by luck or accident."

But how did they do them? These powers, assuming that they exist, do not seem to be sensory. There is no known organ for them. The experiments worked just as well at distances of several hundred miles as they did in the same room. These facts also dispose, in Mr. Wright's opinion, of the attempt to explain telepathy or clairvoyance through any physical theory of radiation. All known forms of radiant energy decline inversely as the square of the distance traversed. Telepathy and clairvoyance do not. But they do vary through physical causes as our other mental powers do. Contrary to widespread opinion, they do not improve when the percipient is asleep or half-asleep, but, on the contrary, when he is most wide-awake and alert. Rhine discovered that a narcotic will invariably lower a percipient's score, while a stimulant will always send it higher. The most reliable performer apparently cannot make a good score unless he tries to do his best.

One conclusion that Wright draws with some confidence is that telepathy and clairvoyance are really one and the same gift. That is, the faculty that "sees" a card face down on a table seems to be exactly the same one that "reads" a thought residing only in another mind. There are several grounds for believing this. So far, for example, the two gifts have been found in every person who enjoys either of them. In every one so far the two have been of equal vigor, almost exactly. Screens, walls, distances, have no effect at all on either. Wright advances from this conclusion to express what he puts forward as no more than the mere "hunch" that other extra-sensory experiences, prophetic dreams, premonitions of disaster, and the like, may also prove to be part of the same faculty. The reader is not asked to accept any of these conclusions unless he finds it necessary, but the evidence that Rhine has piled up must remain impressive.

## Engaging in mental telepathy through the Master Mind principle

In view of Dr. Rhine's announcement in connection with the conditions under which the mind responds to what he terms "extra-sensory" modes of perception, I now feel privileged to add to his testimony by stating that my associates and I have discovered what we believe to be the ideal conditions under which the mind can be stimulated so that the sixth sense, described in Step 10, can be made to function in a practical way.

The conditions to which I refer consist of a close working alliance between me and two members of my staff. Through experimentation and practice, we have discovered how to stimulate our minds (by applying the principle used in connection with the "Invisible Counselors" described in Step 10) so that we can, by a process of blending our three minds into one, find the solution to a great variety of personal problems that are submitted by my clients.

The procedure is very simple. We sit down at a conference table, clearly state the nature of the problem we have under consideration, and then begin discussing it. Each contributes whatever thoughts may occur. The strange thing about this method of mind stimulation is that it places each participant in communication with unknown sources of knowledge definitely outside his own experience.

If you understand the principle described in Step 13 on the Master Mind, you recognize the roundtable procedure here described as being a practical application of the Master Mind.

This method of mind stimulation, through harmonious discussion of definite subjects among three people, illustrates the simplest and most practical use of the Master Mind.

---

**The simplest and most practical use of the Master Mind principle is to engage in a harmonious discussion of a definite subject among members of your Master Mind group.**

---

By adopting and following a similar plan, any student of this philosophy may come into possession of the famous Carnegie formula briefly described in the Author's Preface. If it means nothing to you at this time, mark this page and read it again after you have finished the last step.

*Power* is organized and intelligently directed knowledge.

*Master Mind* is coordination of knowledge and effort, in a spirit of harmony, among two or more people, for the attainment of a definite purpose.

Great power can be accumulated through no other principle than the *Master Mind!*

People take on the nature and the habits and the power of thought of those with whom they associate in a spirit of sympathy and harmony.

# Step 13

# Tap the Power of the *Master Mind*

*Power is organized and intelligently directed knowledge.* As used here, the term "power" refers to *organized effort* sufficient to enable an individual to transmute *desire* into its monetary equivalent. *Organized effort* is the coordinated endeavors of two or more people working toward a *definite* end in a spirit of harmony. The *Master Mind* is the collective intelligence that develops the plan and organizes effort to execute the plan. It is the lens that focuses the light in much the same way as a magnifying glass can be used to focus the rays of the sun to produce intense heat.

*Desires* are inert without sufficient *power* to translate them into *action*. Plans provide the power. The Master Mind supplies the plans. This chapter will describe the method by which an individual may attain and apply *power* through the *Master Mind*.

> *Power is required for the accumulation and retention of money!*

## Identifying sources of knowledge

If power is organized knowledge, acquiring power involves the acquisition of knowledge, which is available through the following sources:

- **Infinite intelligence:** This source of knowledge may be harnessed through the power of creative imagination, as discussed in Chapter 6.
- **General knowledge:** The accumulated experience of humankind (or that portion of it which has been organized and recorded) may be found in any well-equipped public library and on the Internet. An important part of this accumulated experience is taught in public schools and colleges, where it has been classified and organized.
- **Specialized knowledge:** Generalized knowledge that is organized and applied to perform a task, achieve a goal, or create a product. You can develop specialized knowledge yourself or hire it, partner with it, or barter for it, as explained in Step 15.
- **Experiment and research:** In the field of science, and in practically every other walk of life, people gather, classify, and organize new facts daily. This is the source to which one must turn when other sources of knowledge do not provide the information or insight needed. Here, too, the creative imagination must often be used.

---

*Power* is organized and intelligently directed *knowledge*.

---

## Recognizing the limitations of individuals

Knowledge may be converted into *power* by organizing it into definite *plans* and by expressing those plans in terms of *action*. However, by examining the four major sources of knowledge, you realize the difficulty people would have, if they depended upon their efforts alone to assemble the required knowledge and express it through definite, actionable plans. If their plans are comprehensive, and if they contemplate large proportions, they must generally induce others to cooperate with them, before they can inject into those plans the necessary element of *power*.

## Gaining power through the *Master Mind*

The *Master Mind* is the coordination of knowledge and effort, in a spirit of harmony, between two or more people, for the attainment of a definite purpose.

No individual may have great power without availing him or herself of the *Master Mind*. Through the *Master Mind*, you formulate a plan that organizes and applies knowledge for maximum impact in attaining your goal. (For more about organized planning for the purpose of transmuting *desire* into its monetary equivalent, turn to Step 14.) If you carry out these instructions with *persistence* and intelligence and use discrimination in the selection of your *Master Mind group*, you are half way to reaching your objective.

> *Great power can be accumulated through no other principle than that of the Master Mind!*

### The two natures of the *Master Mind*

So you may better understand the "intangible" potentialities of power available to you, through a properly chosen *Master Mind group*, we will here explain the two characteristics of the *Master Mind*:

- **Economic:** Economic advantages may be created by people who surround themselves with the advice, counsel, and personal cooperation of a group of people who are willing to lend wholehearted aid in a spirit of *perfect harmony*. This form of cooperative alliance has been the basis of nearly every great fortune. Your understanding of this great truth may definitely determine your financial status.
- **Psychic:** The human mind is a form of energy, a part of it being spiritual in nature. When the minds of two people are coordinated in a *spirit of harmony*, the spiritual units of energy of each mind form an affinity, which constitutes the psychic phase of the *Master Mind*. When two minds come together, they form a third, invisible intangible force that may be likened to a third mind.

> Mr. Carnegie's *Master Mind group* consisted of a staff of approximately fifty men, with whom he surrounded himself for the *definite purpose* of manufacturing and marketing steel. He attributed his entire fortune to the *power* he accumulated through this *Master Mind*.

## Translation of energy into matter

There are only two known elements in the known universe: energy and matter. According to the scientific laws of the conservation of mass and the conservation of energy, neither energy nor mass can be created or destroyed. They can only be converted or translated into a different form. Einstein's equation E = mc2, which means Energy equals mass times the square of its acceleration, suggests that energy can be converted into mass (matter), and vice versa.

*Energy* is Nature's universal building block, out of which she constructs every form of energy and matter in the universe through a process that only Nature completely understands. Nature's building blocks are available to us in the energy involved in *thinking!*

The brain may be compared to an electric battery. It absorbs energy from the ether, which permeates every atom of matter and fills the entire universe. An individual battery provides energy in proportion to the number and capacity of the cells it contains. A group of batteries provides more energy than a single battery.

The brain functions in a similar fashion. This accounts for the fact that some brains are more powerful than others, and it leads to this significant statement:

A group of brains coordinated (or connected) in a spirit of harmony provides more thought-energy than a single brain, just as a group of electric batteries provides more energy than a single battery.

Through this metaphor, it becomes immediately obvious that the *Master Mind principle* holds the secret of the *power* wielded by people who surround themselves with other intelligent human beings.

There follows, now, another statement that leads still nearer to an understanding of the psychic characteristic of the *Master Mind*:

When a group of individual brains are coordinated and function in harmony, the increased energy created through that alliance becomes available to every individual brain in the group.

## Assemble your *Master Mind* group

When assembling your *Master Mind group*, follow these guidelines:

- **Assemble a diverse group.** Include both male and female members whose knowledge and insight complement, rather than overlap, that of other members.
- **Recruit people who are:**
  - Intelligent
  - Creative
  - Positive
  - Supportive
  - Collaborative
  - Honest
  - Generous
- **Provide some form of compensation.** You may pay them, partner with them, provide a service, offer them a percentage of return on your business, or offer some other form of compensation, but do not expect them to assist you for free, unless they offer to do so.

---

**Remember:** Do not waste their time. Come prepared for meetings and manage meetings efficiently. Valuable members of a *Master Mind group* are typically busy people who are pursuing their own goals.

## Stories that illustrate the *Master Mind* in action

Analyze the record of any person who has accumulated a great fortune and many of those who have accumulated modest fortunes, and you will find that they have either consciously or unconsciously employed the *Master Mind principle*, as in the following success stories.

### Henry Ford

Henry Ford began his business career under the handicap of poverty, illiteracy, and ignorance. Within the inconceivably short period of ten years, Mr. Ford overcame these three handicaps, and within twenty-five years he made himself one of the richest men in America. Connect with this fact the additional knowledge that Mr. Ford's most rapid strides became noticeable from the time he became a personal friend of Thomas A. Edison, and you begin to understand what the influence of one mind upon another can accomplish. Go a step further and consider the fact that Mr. Ford's most outstanding achievements began from the time that he formed the acquaintances of Harvey Firestone, John Burroughs, and Luther Burbank, (each a man of great brain capacity), and you have further evidence that *power* may be produced through friendly alliance of minds.

There is little if any doubt that Henry Ford was one of the best-informed men in the business and industrial world. The question of his wealth needs no discussion. Analyze Mr. Ford's intimate personal friends, some of whom have already been mentioned, and you will be prepared to understand the following statement:

*People take on the nature and the habits and the **power of thought** of those with whom they associate in a spirit of sympathy and harmony.*

Henry Ford whipped poverty, illiteracy, and ignorance by allying himself with great minds whose vibrations of thought he absorbed into his own mind. Through his association with Edison, Burbank, Burroughs, and Firestone, Ford added to his own brainpower the sum and substance of the intelligence, experience, knowledge, and spiritual forces of these four men. Moreover, he appropriated and made use of the *Master Mind principle* through the methods of procedure described in this book.

This principle is available to you!

---

**People take on the nature and the habits and the power of thought of those with whom they associate in a spirit of sympathy and harmony.**

---

### President Franklin D. Roosevelt

President Franklin Roosevelt brought the best minds of the country to Washington to form a *Master Mind group* he called his "brain trust." During and after World War II, *Master Mind groups* called "think tanks" were frequently called upon by leaders of government and industry to help deal with critical problems.

### Mahatma Gandhi

Perhaps the majority of those who have heard of Gandhi, look upon him as merely an eccentric little man, who dressed like a pauper and made trouble for the British Government.

In reality, Gandhi was not eccentric, but *he was the most powerful man of his generation* (based on the number of his followers and their faith in their leader). Moreover, he was probably the most powerful man who ever lived. His power was passive, but it was real.

Let us study the method by which he attained his stupendous *power*. It may be explained in a few words. He came by *power* through inducing over two hundred million people to coordinate, with mind and body, in a spirit of *harmony*, for a *definite purpose*.

In brief, Gandhi accomplished a *miracle*, for it is a miracle when two hundred million people can be induced, not forced, to cooperate in a spirit of *harmony*, for a limitless time. If you doubt that this is a miracle, try to induce *any two people* to cooperate in a spirit of harmony for any length of time.

Every person who manages a business knows what a difficult matter it is to get employees to work together in a spirit even remotely resembling *harmony*.

The list of the chief sources from which *power* may be attained is, as you have seen, headed by *infinite intelligence*. When two or more people coordinate in a spirit of *harmony* and work toward a definite objective, they place themselves in position, through that alliance, to absorb power directly from the great universal storehouse of Infinite Intelligence. This is the greatest of all sources of *power*. It is the source to which the genius turns. It is the source to which every great leader turns (whether conscious of the fact or not).

The other three major sources from which the knowledge necessary for the accumulation of *power* may be obtained are no more reliable than our five senses. The senses are not always reliable. Infinite Intelligence *does not err*.

### Andrew Grove

Some of the best sources for creating your own *Master Mind group* are your employees. Andrew Grove, the extremely successful CEO of Intel Corporation did this. Grove works with a group of technical, marketing, financial, and administrative men and women as a team in an informal work environment. There are no private offices or special parking spaces or other privileges for executives. Employees have a generous stock option plan so that if the company makes money and the stock rises, they can share in the gains.

Although the team may appear to be casual, they follow Grove's lead of being very demanding on themselves. When Intel faced a crisis in 1976, the teams willingly put in extra effort and more work hours and did whatever was necessary to solve the problems. On another occasion, it was discovered that the Intel Pentium chip had a minor defect that would affect an insignificant number of operations. Grove's decision to replace the Pentiums at a cost of $475 million rather than deliver a product that was not perfect was fully endorsed by his colleagues.

Grove encouraged his people to work in small, autonomous units in which everyone understands the system and his or her role in it. Each person contributes his or her knowledge, expertise, and creativity. Team members are trained and motivated to produce to the best of their capacity. When crises arise, the team willingly puts in the extra time, energy, and brainpower to solve the problems.

## Ross Perot

Ross Perot's attitude exemplifies the power of tough-minded commitment—not only his own, but that of the *Master Mind* with which he surrounded himself. He had a burning desire for wealth, and he achieved it.

Before starting Electronic Data Systems (EDS), Perot had been the top sales person at IBM. He was cautioned that leaving IBM to start as company from scratch was a mistake. This did not faze Perot. He was inspired by a vision of what could be. His success clearly demonstrates that by sticking to your dream and transmitting that dream to a team of experts—a *Master Mind*—who have the know-how to help make it a realization leads to success and wealth.

Perot firmly believes that commitment can accomplish miracles. This was exemplified when EDS competed for one of the largest contracts in the computer industry. Two companies, IBM and EDS, were the contestants. IBM was far richer and had in its staff a more experienced and knowledgeable group of specialists. EDS had a small but dedicated team.

Perot recalls,

*About 30 days into the competition, I walked into the room, and our 15 guys were saying, "Gee, we probably can't win, but it will be great experience." I didn't jump up and down and chew people out. I just walked to the blackboard and wrote down the seven criteria by which we would be judged. And in a nice low voice said, "We are going to beat them seven to zero." That's the day we won.*

Perot commented that the raises, the bonuses, the stock options, and thousands of new jobs winning this project created were, of course, the tangible rewards of achieving this coup. However, he believes that more important was the immense satisfaction of knowing that by their hard work and creativity, they beat the best in the world. That's what makes a company great—a team working together as a *Master Mind* to beat the opposition.

## Reaping the profits of the power gained

When money comes in quantities known as "the big money," it flows to the one who accumulates it, as easily as water flows downhill. There exists a great unseen stream of *power*, which may be compared to a river; except that one side flows in one direction, carrying all who get into that side of the stream onward and upward to *wealth*. The other side flows in the opposite direction, carrying all who are unfortunate enough to get into it (and unable to extricate themselves from it) downward to misery and *poverty*.

Every person who has accumulated a great fortune has recognized the existence of this stream of life. It consists of one's *thinking process*. The positive emotions of thought form the side of the stream that carries one to fortune. The negative emotions form the side that carries one down to poverty.

This carries a thought of stupendous importance to the person who is following this book with the object of accumulating a fortune.

If you are in the side of the stream of *power* that leads to poverty, this may serve as an oar by which you may propel yourself over into the other side of the stream. It can serve you *only* through application and use. Merely reading and passing judgment on it, either one way or another, will in no way benefit you.

Some people undergo the experience of alternating between the positive and negative sides of the stream, being at times on the positive side, and at times on the negative side. The Wall Street crash of '29 and the financial crisis of 2008 swept millions of people from the positive to the negative side of the stream. These millions struggled—some of them in desperation and fear—to get back to the positive side of the stream. This book was written especially for those millions.

Poverty and riches often change places. Poverty may, and generally does, voluntarily take the place of riches. When riches take the place of poverty, the change is usually brought about through well-conceived and carefully executed *plans*. Poverty needs no plan. It needs no one to aid it, because it is bold and ruthless. Riches are shy and timid. They have to be attracted.

*Anybody* can *wish* for riches, and most people do, but only a few know that a definite plan combined with a *burning desire* for wealth are the only dependable means of accumulating wealth.

You cannot accumulate money without a practical, workable plan.

# Step 14

# Settle on a Plan

Whether you have an idea and must organize a workforce to bring it to fruition or you have specialized knowledge (services) to sell, you must have a plan in place to transmute your desire or vision into its monetary equivalent. In this chapter, you discover how to use your Master Mind group to develop a plan and to change or adjust plans if they are not producing the desired results. This chapter also provides guidance on how to market the services you offer, so you can charge top dollar for those services.

---

**Remember:** Plans are created in the *imagination*—
the Workshop of the Mind. For more about tapping
the power of the imagination, see Step 9.

---

## Create a plan

Step 5 presented six steps for transmuting *desire* into its monetary equivalent. In the fourth step, you were instructed to "Create a definite plan for carrying out your desire, and begin at once to put this plan into action." However, no guidance was provided on *how to create a plan*. Here is that guidance.

---

The most intelligent person living cannot succeed in accumulating money—nor in any other undertaking—without plans that are practical and workable.

---

## Assemble your planning committee: Your *Master Mind group*

To create a viable plan, assemble and work with a planning committee (*Master Mind group*), as follows:

1. Ally yourself with a group of as many people as you may need for the creation and carrying out of your plan or plans for the accumulation of money, making use of the *Master Mind* principle described in Step 13. As you select members for your *Master Mind* group, endeavor to choose those who refuse to accept defeat.

2. Before forming your *Master Mind group*, decide what advantages and benefits you may offer the individual members of your group in return for their cooperation. No one will work indefinitely without some form of compensation. No intelligent person will either request or expect another to work without adequate compensation, although this may not always be in the form of money

3. Arrange to meet with the members of your *Master Mind group* at least twice a week and more often if possible, until you have jointly perfected the necessary plan or plans for the accumulation of money.

4. Maintain *perfect harmony* between yourself and every member of your *Master Mind group*. If you fail to carry out this instruction to the letter, you may expect to meet with failure. The *Master Mind* principle cannot obtain where *perfect harmony* does not prevail.

Keep in mind these facts:
- First: You are engaged in an undertaking of major importance to you. To ensure success, you must have plans that are faultless.
- Second: You must have the advantage of the experience, education, native ability, and imagination of other minds. This is in harmony with the methods followed by every person who has accumulated a great fortune.

No individual has sufficient experience, education, native ability, and knowledge to ensure the accumulation of a great fortune without the cooperation of other people. Every plan you adopt in your endeavor to accumulate wealth should be the joint creation of yourself and every other member of your *Master Mind group*. You may originate your own plans, either in whole or in part, but *see that those plans are checked and approved by the members of your Master Mind group*.

---

*No individual has sufficient experience, education, native ability, and knowledge to ensure the accumulation of a great fortune without the cooperation of other people.*

---

### Address the key the components of any plan

Plans vary depending on the nature of the industry and business and the product(s) or service(s) you intend to market. You and your *Master Mind group* must define the details. However, your plan should address the following areas:

- Goal or mission
- Description of your business and the product(s) and/or service(s) it offers (if you are your business, a description of what you offer)
- Statement of what makes you or your business unique and better
- SWOT analysis highlighting your or your business's Strengths and Weaknesses along with marketplace Opportunities (unmet or underserved needs) and Threats (from competition, for example) OR business intelligence (intel) exposing a unique and significant opportunity with little or no competition in the marketplace
- Description of your management team (*Master Mind group*) and the qualities and accomplishments that make them uniquely qualified to execute the plan
- Plans to market the product(s) and/or service(s) being offered
- Financial analysis that covers start-up and operating costs, revenue projections, and cash flow
- Specialized knowledge required to offer the product(s) or service(s), market them, deliver them to the marketplace, and run the business (this is either knowledge you have or must obtain through other means, as explained in Step 15)

## Be persistent and adjust the plan as necessary

If the first plan you adopt does not succeed, replace it with a new plan. If this new plan fails to work, replace it with another and so on, until you find a plan that *does work*. Right here is the point at which the majority of people meet with failure, because of their lack of *persistence* in creating new plans to take the place of those that fail.

---

**Remember:** Temporary defeat is not permanent failure. It may only mean that your plans have not been sound. Build other plans. Start over.

---

We see people who have accumulated great fortunes, but we often recognize only their triumph, overlooking the temporary defeats that they had to surmount before they achieved their goals. Here are a few examples:

- Thomas A. Edison "failed" ten thousand times before he perfected the incandescent electric light bulb; that is, he met with temporary defeat ten thousand times, before his efforts were crowned with success.
- James J. Hill met with temporary defeat when he first endeavored to raise the necessary capital to build a railroad from the East to the West, but he turned defeat into victory through new plans.
- Henry Ford met with temporary defeat, not only at the beginning of his automobile career, but after he had gone far toward the top. He created new plans and continued marching on to financial victory.

*No follower of this philosophy can reasonably expect to accumulate a fortune without experiencing temporary defeat.* When defeat comes, accept it as a signal that your plans are not sound, rebuild those plans, and set sail once more toward your coveted goal. If you give up before your goal has been reached, you are a "quitter."

---

*A quitter never wins, and a winner never quits.*
Write this sentence on a piece of paper in letters an inch high, and place it where you will see it every night before you go to sleep and every morning before you go to work.

---

## Plan the sale of services

Nearly all great fortunes began in the form of compensation for personal services or from the sale of *ideas*. If you do not have property or ideas to transmute into riches, then all you can offer are your *personal services* or *specialized knowledge*. Those who have lost their fortunes, and those who are just beginning to earn money, have nothing but personal services to offer in return for riches; therefore, it is essential that they have available the practical information needed to market their services to their best advantage.

The remainder of this chapter has been given over to a description of ways and means of marketing personal services. The information here conveyed will be of practical help to any person having any form of personal services to market. It will be particularly helpful to those aiming to market their services as business or industrial executives.

If you do not have property or ideas to transmute into riches, then all you can offer are your *personal services*.

## Know when and how to apply for a position

The information described here is the net result of many years of experience during which thousands of individuals were helped to market their services effectively. It can, therefore, be relied upon as sound and practical.

## Do your homework

Before applying for a position, do your homework to identify positions you find attractive and are qualified for and to find out ways you can present yourself as a valuable new hire to prospective employers and recruiters:

1. Decide *exactly* what kind of a job you want. If the job doesn't already exist, perhaps you can create it.
2. Choose the company or individual for or with whom you wish to work.
3. Study your prospective employer, as to policies, personnel, chances of advancement, competitors, and clients. Look for opportunities the prospective employer may be missing out on or ways the business could be improved.
4. By analysis of yourself and your talents and capabilities, figure *what you can offer*, and plan ways and means of giving advantages, services, improvements, and ideas that you believe you can successfully deliver.
5. Forget about "getting a job." Forget whether or not there is an opening. Concentrate on what you can *give* that would make you valuable enough to hire.

6. Once you have your plan in mind, arrange with an experienced writer to help you put it on paper in neat form, and in full detail. (See the later section "Information to be supplied in a written résumé" for details.)
7. Present it to the proper person with authority to make the decision. Every company is looking for people who can give something of value in the form of ideas, services, or connections. Every company has room for the person who has a definite plan of action to the advantage of that company.

This approach may take extra days or weeks, but the difference in income, recognition, and advancement will save years of hard work at low pay. It has many advantages, the main one being that it often saves from one to five years of time in reaching a chosen career and income goal.

---

*Every person who starts, or "gets in" half way up the ladder, does so by deliberate and careful planning, (except, of course, the Boss' son).*

---

## Leverage media through which services may be marketed

Experience has proved that the following media offer the most direct and effective methods of bringing the buyer and seller of personal services together:

- **Networking:** Most people find work through networking connections, and networking has never been easier. Use websites, such as LinkedIn, Facebook, and Twitter to create and grow your network and tap its power to find openings that match your knowledge, skills, passions, and goals. Employers tend to hire people they know or applicants referred by people they know, so, when possible, approach prospective employers through a mutual acquaintance.

- **Social media:** Develop a profile on websites such as LinkedIn, Facebook, and Twitter that accurately reflects your qualifications and accomplishments and makes you an attractive target for prospective employers and recruiters. Become involved in relevant discussion groups, where you can demonstrate your specialized knowledge and other qualities that an employer is likely to value. You may even create and manage your own blog to become a thought-leader in your field.
- **Applications, cover letters, and résumés:** When applying for a position, focus on the prospective employer's needs and how you are qualified to meet or exceed those needs. Instead of highlighting what you *know* (skills and knowledge), highlight specific ways you helped past employers and what you can *do* for the prospective employer. Prepare your cover letter, résumé, and application with expert guidance. (See the next section to determine the type of information to provide.)
- **Recruiters:** Recruiters are constantly seeking top-quality talent in a variety of fields, so they can "sell" talented individuals to employers on commission. Use social media, as described above, to make yourself an attractive and easy-to-find talent online.
- **Freelancer websites:** More and more businesses hire on-demand, so they can scale up and scale down their work-

force to meet changing demands. You can now market your freelance services to prospective employers on a host of websites, including Elance (www.elance.com), Fiverr (www.fiverr.com), Freelancer (www.freelancer.com), Guides.co (guides.co), HourlyNerd (hourlynerd.com), and Silkshare (www.skillshare.com).

- **Paid advertising:** Advertising in newspapers, trade journals, magazines, and on the Internet may generate leads. Seek advice from an expert who understands how to prepare the advertising copy in a way that is most effective in promoting your value.

- **Application in person:** In some industries and situations, applying in-person is most effective. Even when applying in person, however, you should bring a neatly typed cover letter and résumé that presents your qualifications in writing. This provides the prospective employer with documentation to refer to in the future and to share with others who may be involved in making the hiring decision.

---

Networking is a crucial component to effectively marketing your services. You must *connect with people and maintain relationships* in whatever field you choose to pursue.

---

## Prepare your résumé

Prepare your résumé as carefully as a lawyer would prepare the brief of a case to be tried in court. Unless you are experienced in preparing résumés, consult an expert. Successful merchants employ people who understand the art and the psychology of advertising to present the merits of their merchandise. One who has personal services for sale should do the same.

---

**Tip:** Read the job posting carefully and be sure to highlight in your cover letter and resume the experience, skills, and knowledge you have that match up with the employer's specific needs, as described in the job posting.

---

The following information should appear in the résumé:

- **Specific position being applied for:** Avoid application for a position without describing *exactly* what particular position you seek. Never apply for "just a position," which indicates you lack specialized qualifications.
- **Your qualifications for the position:** Give full details as to the reason you believe you are qualified for the particular position you seek. This is *the most important detail of your application*. It determines, more than anything else, what consideration you receive.
- **Experience:** If you have experience in connection with positions similar to the one you seek, describe it fully and state the names and addresses of former employers. Be sure to bring out clearly any special experience that qualifies you for the position you seek.
- **Applicable skills:** List skills you have that are needed to perform the advertised job. Your prospective employer is interested more in what you are able to do than what you know.
- **Accomplishments:** Provide at least three concrete examples of how you made money or saved money for previous employers or improved the business in some way; for

example, by completing a project ahead of schedule or making a process more efficient.
- **Education:** State briefly, but definitely, what schooling you have had and in what subjects you specialized in school, giving your reasons for that specialization.
- **References:** Wise employers will check references from previous jobs to verify your identity, knowledge, skills, and performance. Line up your references in advance and provide at least three references and their contact information. References may include any of the following:
  - Former employers or supervisors
  - Teachers under whom you studied
  - Prominent people whose judgment is reliable
- **Knowledge of your prospective employer's business:** Before applying for a position, do sufficient research to familiarize yourself thoroughly with that business and the industry in which it operates. In your cover letter and during the interview, demonstrate your knowledge and ask intelligent questions to show that you have done your homework. You may even have ideas about how to improve the prospective employer's business. In any event, it shows that you can take the initiative and care about the business and not just the job it offers.

*Offer to work on probation* for a week, or a month, or for a sufficient length of time to enable your prospective employer to judge your value *without pay*. This may appear to be a radical suggestion, but experience has proven that it seldom fails to win at least a trial. If you are *sure of your qualifications*, a trial is all you need. Incidentally, such an offer indicates that you have confidence in your ability to fill the position you seek. It is most convincing. If your offer is accepted and you make good on it, more than likely you will be paid for your probation period. Make clear the fact that your offer is based upon:

- Your confidence in your ability to fill the position
- Your confidence in your prospective employer's decision to employ you after trial
- Your *determination* to have the position you seek

---

**Remember:** It is not the lawyer who knows the most law, but the one who best prepares the case, who wins. If your "case" is properly prepared and presented, your victory will have been more than half won at the outset.

---

Do not be afraid of making your résumé too long. Employers are just as much interested in purchasing the services of well-qualified applicants as you are in securing employment. In fact, the success of most successful employers is due, primarily, to their ability to select well-qualified employees. They want all the information available.

---

**Remember:** Neatness in the preparation of your résumé indicates that you *care* and that you *attend to details*. I have helped to prepare résumés for clients that were so striking and out of the ordinary that they resulted in the employment of the applicant without a personal interview.

---

Once the résumé is completed, have it typed on the finest paper you can obtain. Carefully check the spelling and grammar. Follow these instructions to the letter, improving upon them wherever your imagination suggests.

Successful sales people groom themselves with care. They understand that first impressions are lasting. Your résumé is your sales representative. Give it a good suit of clothes, so it will stand out in bold contrast to anything your prospective employer ever saw in the way of an application for a position. If the position you seek is worth having, it is worth pursuing with care. Moreover, if you sell yourself to an employer in a manner that impresses him or her with your individuality, you probably will receive more money for your services from the very start, than you would if you applied for employment in the usual conventional way.

### View your job as a partnership

When you are in the business of selling your services, you would do best to view your job as a partnership in which you and your employer partner, as colleagues, to serve the needs of the client or customer.

In the past, employers and employees have bartered among themselves, driving the best bargains they could with one another, not considering that in the final analysis they were, in reality, *bargaining at the expense of the third party, the customers they served.*

---

The time will come when the "Golden Rule," not the "Rule of Gold," will be the dominating factor in the marketing of merchandise as well as personal services.

---

In the future both employers and employees will recognize that they are *no longer privileged to drive bargains at the expense of those they serve.* The real employer of the future will be the customer. This should be kept uppermost in mind by every person seeking to market personal services effectively.

"Courtesy" and "service" are the watch-words of merchandising today and apply to the person who is marketing personal services even more directly than to the employer whom he serves, because, in the final analysis, both the employer and his employee are *employed by the customers they serve.* If they fail to serve well, they pay by the loss of their privilege of serving.

---

> Yesterday's "go-getter" has been supplanted by today's "go-giver." The provider who gives the most value is in highest demand and attracts the highest compensation for the services provided.

---

## Know your "QQS" rating

It is up to *you* to sell your own personal services. The *quality* and the *quantity* of service rendered, and the *spirit* in which it is rendered, determine to a large extent the price and the duration of employment. To market personal services effectively, (which means a permanent market, at a satisfactory price, under pleasant conditions), one must adopt and follow the "QQS" formula which means that *quality*, plus *quantity*, plus the proper *spirit* of cooperation, equals perfect marketing of service. Remember the "QQS" formula, but do more—*apply it as a habit!*

Let us analyze the formula to make sure we understand exactly what it means:

- *Quality of service* shall be construed to mean the performance of every detail, in connection with your position,

in the most efficient manner possible, with the object of greater efficiency always in mind.
- *Quantity of service* shall be understood to mean the *habit* of rendering all the service of which you are capable, at all times, with the purpose of increasing the amount of service rendered as greater skill is developed through practice and experience. Emphasis is again placed on the word *habit*.
- *Spirit of service* shall be construed to mean the *habit* of agreeable, harmonious conduct that will induce cooperation from associates and fellow employees.

Adequacy of *quality* and *quantity* of service is not sufficient to maintain a permanent market for your services. The conduct, or the *spirit* in which you deliver service, is a strong determining factor in connection with both the price you receive and the duration of employment.

---

**QQS formula:** Quality + Quantity + Spirit of cooperation = perfect marketing of service

---

Andrew Carnegie stressed this point more than others in connection with his description of the factors that lead to success in the marketing of personal services. He emphasized again and again the necessity for *harmonious conduct*. He stressed the fact that he would not retain any person, no matter how great a *quantity* or how efficient the *quality* of his or her work, unless that person worked in a spirit of *harmony*. Mr. Carnegie insisted upon everybody being *agreeable*. To prove that he placed a high value upon this quality, he permitted many people who conformed to his standards to become very wealthy. Those who did not conform had to make room for others.

The importance of a pleasing personality has been stressed, because it is a factor that enables one to render service in the proper *spirit*. If one has a personality which *pleases* and renders service in a spirit of *harmony*, these assets often make up for deficiencies in both the *quality* and the *quantity* of service one renders. Nothing, however, can be *successfully substituted for pleasing conduct*.

### To earn more, be worth more

When you sell personal services (your brains), you are subject to *exactly the same rules* of conduct as the merchant who sells merchandise. Your employer is your customer, and to maintain the privilege of serving your customer, you must supply merchandise (your services) that your customer finds valuable enough to pay the amount you charge. If your QQS rating does not warrant the fees you charge, you will not be in business very long. We emphasize this point, because the majority of people who live by the sale of personal services make the mistake of considering themselves free from the rules of conduct and the responsibilities attached to those who are engaged in marketing commodities. As a result, they may expect higher compensation than their services are worth.

Before you start to negotiate for a raise, seek employment elsewhere, or set fees for your services *be sure that you offer something of value commensurate with the compensation you expect*. It is one thing to *want* money—everyone wants more—but it is something entirely different to be *worth more!* Many people mistake their *wants* for their *just dues*. Your financial requirements or wants have nothing whatever to do with your *worth*. Your value is established entirely by your ability to render useful service or your capacity to induce others to render such service.

The folly of ignorance in this matter was displayed by a young man who applied to the manager of a well-known business for a position. He made a very good impression until the manager asked him what salary he expected. He replied that he had no fixed sum in mind (lack of a definite aim). The manager then said, "We will pay you all you are worth, after we try you out for a week."

"I will not accept it," the applicant replied, "because *I am getting more than that where I am now employed.*" He knew that his current employer was paying him more than he was worth! Otherwise, he would have jumped at the opportunity to prove the value of his services and command higher compensation.

---

If you *want* money, be *worth more money!*

---

## Take inventory of yourself: Twenty-eight questions

Annual self-analysis is an essential in the effective marketing of personal services, as is annual inventory in merchandising. Moreover, the yearly analysis should disclose a *decrease in faults* and an increase in *virtues*. One moves forward, stands still, or goes backward in life. One's object should be, of course, to progress. Annual self-analysis will disclose whether progress has been made and, if so, how much. It will also disclose any regression. The effective marketing of personal services requires one to move forward even if progress is slow.

Perform your annual self-analysis at the end of each year, so you can include in your New Year's Resolutions any improvements that the analysis indicates should be made. Take this inventory by asking yourself the following questions and by checking your answers with the aid of someone who will not permit you to deceive yourself as to their accuracy:

1. Have I attained the goal that I established as my objective for this year? (You should work with a definite yearly objective to be attained as a part of your major life objective.)
2. Have I delivered service of the best possible *quality* of which I was capable, or could I have improved any part of this service?
3. Have I delivered service in the greatest possible *quantity* of which I was capable?
4. Has the spirit of my conduct been harmonious and cooperative at all times?
5. Have I permitted the habit of *procrastination* to decrease my efficiency and, if so, to what extent?
6. Have I improved my *personality* and, if so, in what ways?
7. Have I been *persistent* in following my plans through to completion?
8. Have I reached *decisions promptly and definitely* on all occasions?
9. Have I permitted any one or more of the six basic fears to decrease my efficiency?
10. Have I been either "over-cautious" or "under-cautious?"
11. Has my relationship with my associates in work been pleasant or unpleasant? If it has been unpleasant, has the fault been partly or wholly mine?

12. Have I dissipated any of my energy through lack of *concentration* of effort?
13. Have I been open-minded and tolerant in connection with all subjects?
14. In what way have I improved my ability to render service?
15. Have I been intemperate in any of my habits?
16. Have I expressed, either openly or secretly, any form of *egotism*?
17. Has my conduct toward my associates been such that it has induced them to *respect* me?
18. Have my opinions and *decisions* been based upon guesswork or on accuracy of analysis and *thought*?
19. Have I followed the habit of budgeting my time, my expenses, and my income, and have I been conservative in these budgets?
20. How much time have I devoted to *unprofitable* effort, which I might have used to better advantage?
21. How may I *re-budget* my time and change my habits so I will be more efficient during the coming year?
22. Have I been guilty of any conduct that was not approved by my conscience?
23. In what ways have I rendered *more and better service* than I was paid to render?
24. Have I been unfair to anyone and, if so, in what way?
25. If I had been the purchaser of my own services for the year, would I be satisfied with my purchase?
26. Am I in the right vocation and, if not, why not?
27. Has the purchaser of my services been satisfied with the service I have rendered and, if not, why not?

28. What is my present rating on the fundamental principles of success? (Make this rating fairly and frankly, and have it checked by someone who is courageous enough to do it accurately.)

---

The effective marketing of personal services requires one to move forward even if progress is slow.

---

Complete assimilation and understanding of the information here conveyed will be helpful in marketing one's own services, and it also helps one to become more analytical and capable of judging people. The information is priceless to personnel directors, employment managers, and other executives charged with selecting employees and maintaining efficient organizations.

An *idea* combined with a *plan* and the *specialized knowledge* to execute the plan yields riches.

Knowledge is power only when organized into a definite plan of action for achieving a definite goal.

Specialized knowledge does *not* have to be in the possession of the person who accumulates the fortune.

# Step 15

# Put Specialized Knowledge to Work for You

Knowledge itself isn't power, and it is of little use in the accumulation of money. Knowledge becomes power only if and when *it is organized into definite plans of action and directed to a definite purpose.* Furthermore, knowledge is either *general* or *specialized:*

- **General knowledge** is information, description, or explanation that expands one's understanding.
- **Specialized knowledge** is generalized knowledge that is organized and applied to perform a task, achieve a goal, or create a product.

Consider these two forms of knowledge as they apply to medicine. In medical school, students first obtain *general knowledge* about human anatomy and physiology, infectious agents, genetics, and so forth. Specialized knowledge is gained in clinical settings, such as during internships, when medical students learn how to apply their general knowledge to treat patients and cure illness. Medical students increase their specialized knowledge during a residency period, during which they practice their chosen specialty in a supervised setting.

---

Knowledge becomes power only if and when it is organized into definite plans of action and directed to a definite purpose. *Knowledge* will not attract money unless it is organized and intelligently directed through practical *plans of action* to the accumulation of money.

---

If you have *imagination*, this chapter may present you with an idea sufficient to serve as the beginning of the riches you desire.

## Two ways to earn money

Before you can be sure of your ability to transmute *desire* into its monetary equivalent, you will require *specialized knowledge* of the service, merchandise, or profession that you intend to offer in return for fortune. Perhaps you may need much more specialized knowledge than you have the ability or the inclination to acquire, and if this should be true, you may bridge your weakness through the aid of your *Master Mind group*—individuals who have the specialized knowledge that you lack (see Step 13 for more about forming a *Master Mind group*). Generally speaking, there are two ways to earn money:

- Sell your specialized knowledge to someone who needs it and is willing to pay for it.

- Think and grow rich by coming up with an *idea*, devising a *plan* to make money, and then obtaining (perhaps buying, bartering for, or partnering with) the *specialized knowledge* to execute your plan.

The accumulation of great fortunes calls for *power*, and power is acquired through highly organized and intelligently directed specialized knowledge, but that *knowledge does not necessarily have to be in the possession of the person who accumulates the fortune.*

This should give hope and encouragement to the individual with ambition but without the necessary education or specialized knowledge to accumulate a fortune. People sometimes go through life suffering from inferiority complexes, because they lack formal education. The person who can organize and direct a *Master Mind group* of people who possess knowledge useful in the accumulation of money is just as much an educated person as anyone in the group.

---

*Specialized knowledge* is among the most plentiful and the cheapest forms of service which may be had!

---

## Ideas give knowledge a purpose

*Ideas* are thoughts that give knowledge a definite purpose. They are the first step on the journey to *think and grow rich*, the seeds from which great fortunes have grown. Specialized knowledge is far more abundant than ideas, which is why ideas are more valuable. A person who has an *idea*, the *burning desire* to bring it into being, and a solid *plan* (supplied by Infinite Intelligence) can easily access the specialized knowledge necessary to bring what is imagined into being. An *idea* is capable of yielding an income far greater than that of the average doctor, lawyer, or engineer whose specialized knowledge required several years in college.

---

The *idea* is the main thing. Specialized knowledge may be found just around the corner—any corner!

---

By applying the principle of *specialized knowledge*, a few people with suitable talent could form an alliance and have a paying business very quickly. One would need to be a fair writer, with a flair for advertising and selling, one handy at graphic design, and one "rainmaker" who is talented at generating new business. If one person possessed all these abilities, he or she might carry on the business alone, until it became too big for one person to handle. If you have the *imagination*, and seek a more profitable outlet for your personal services, this suggestion may be the stimulus for which you have been searching.

## How to acquire specialized knowledge

First of all, decide the sort of specialized knowledge you require and the purpose for which it is needed. To a large extent the goal toward which you are working determines the type(s) of specialized knowledge you need. To acquire the specialized knowledge you do not have but need to execute your plan, consider the following options:

- Tap your existing knowledge and experience
- Obtain it yourself by taking courses (at a college, university, or trade school), reading (books, magazines, or journals), researching online, and asking questions

- Buy it by hiring people who have it to work for you part or full time or on contract
- Partner with someone who has the knowledge, skills, and other resources you lack
- Barter for it, perhaps by offering a percentage of your profits
- Work or serve for it by volunteering, working as an intern, or working in some capacity for a business in the industry in which you desire to pursue wealth

The Internet has made specialized knowledge readily available. You can find and connect with people online who, collectively, have all the specialized knowledge you need to execute your plan, whether you need someone to research potentially lucrative business opportunities, incorporate your business, patent an idea, create a website, design and manufacture a product, or provide some other service. You can even connect with business consultants for guidance and insight. Old-school networking also works wonders; connect with entrepreneurial-minded individuals locally to exchange specialized knowledge and skills and perhaps collaborate on business ideas.

## Advice for students entering college and their parents

If you are a high school student or graduate planning to continue your education at an institution of higher learning (a college or university), decide how you will apply the knowledge you seek before choosing a major or course of study. The faculties of the great universities possess, in the aggregate, practically every form of general knowledge known to civilization. They impart knowledge, but they rarely teach their students *how to organize and use knowledge after they acquire it.* This is one of the main reasons why college graduates often have trouble securing gainful employment after they graduate.

Year after year college placement counselors report that recruiters who come to their campuses are chiefly interested in hiring students who have majored in a specialized field such as business management, computer science, mathematics, chemistry, and other areas which prepare them to move rapidly into productive jobs, rather than the liberal arts students who have broader but unspecialized schooling.

If you are uncertain of how you plan to apply your knowledge after you acquire it, consider postponing your entry into higher education until you have a clearer vision of your ultimate goal. In the meantime, work toward clarifying your vision:

- Read this book and perform the exercises to form a vision of *what you want* or *what service or product you want to offer* in exchange for money. There is no lower or upper age limit on the ability to *think and grow rich*. The exercises in this book are useful for everybody.
- Take a career aptitude test to identify your strengths and weaknesses and identify careers and skills you're best suited for and interested in. Many high schools and colleges provide such tests or similar assessments. However, *do not allow such assessments to discourage you from pursuing any goal you truly desire.*
- Explore a variety of fields, both those that require college degrees and those that do not. Give your imagination the

information it needs to formulate thoughts about what is possible.
- Read as much as possible about fields that interest you.
- Talk with people currently engaged in the line of work that interests you to gauge current and future opportunity potential and start to develop a plan for entering the field you desire.
- Check out the *Bureau of Labor Statistics Occupation Outlook Handbook* at www.bls.gov/ooh to find out the projected demand for jobs in a wide variety of fields. You can browse occupations by category or by highest paying, fastest growing, or most new jobs created.

---

The right career or field for you is a blend of what you are good at, what you have a passion for, and the specialized knowledge that is in high demand. If you are not qualified to perform a service, you will not be successful. If you have no passion for it, you will not be happy. If it is not in high demand, opportunities will be limited or pay will be low.

---

## Become a lifelong learner

Successful people, in all callings, never stop acquiring specialized knowledge related to their major purpose, business, or profession. Those who are not successful usually make the mistake of believing that their education ended upon graduation. However, the most valuable aspects of higher education are the curiosity it nurtures (the eagerness to learn) and learning and thinking skills—the ability to read and comprehend and make educated judgments about the truth and value of the information presented.

---

> The person who stops seeking knowledge merely because he has finished school is forever hopelessly doomed to mediocrity, regardless of his calling.

---

The ever-changing economic conditions in our society have made it necessary for thousands of people to find new sources of income. For the majority of these, the solution to their problem may be found only by acquiring specialized knowledge. Many will be forced to change their occupations entirely. When a merchant finds that a certain line of merchandise is not selling, he must find another that is in demand. Likewise, if you find that your services are no longer in demand or are not selling for a price that meets your financial needs or desire, you must find another service to provide that's in higher demand and shorter supply.

If you need to acquire new specialized knowledge, you can find plenty of educational opportunities, including these:

- Continuing education courses at community colleges and universities.
- Degree or certification programs at online colleges and universities.
- Massive open online courses (MOOC) by education providers such as Coursera (coursera.org), EdX (edx.org), Lynda (lynda.com), and Udacity (udacity.com). Search for more on The Mind Unleashed web site (themindunleashed.org).
- On-the-job training through internships and apprenticeships.

> The way of success is the way of continuous pursuit of knowledge.

## Stories of individuals who harnessed the power of specialized knowledge

Throughout history, people with and without formal education have managed, through their ability to think and to apply specialized knowledge, to achieve great feats and acquire riches. Here are just a few stories that illustrate the power that can be wielded through the proper application of specialized knowledge.

### Henry Ford: Specialized knowledge at the press of a button

An *educated person* is not necessarily one who has an abundance of general or specialized knowledge. Educated people have developed the faculties of their minds that they may acquire anything they want, or its equivalent, without violating the rights of others. Henry Ford comes well within the meaning of this definition of "educated person."

> *Educated people* have developed the faculties of their minds that they may acquire anything they want, or its equivalent, without violating the rights of others.

During the First World War, a Chicago newspaper published certain editorials in which, among other statements, Henry Ford was called "an ignorant pacifist." Mr. Ford objected to the statements and brought suit against the paper for libeling him. When the suit was tried in the courts, the attorneys for the paper pleaded justification and placed Mr. Ford on the witness stand for the purpose of proving to the jury that he was ignorant. The attorneys asked Mr. Ford a great variety of questions, all of them intended to prove, by his own evidence, that while he might possess considerable specialized knowledge pertaining to the manufacture of automobiles, he was ignorant in the general knowledge imparted by most educational institutions at the time.

Mr. Ford was plied with such questions as "Who was Benedict Arnold?" and "How many soldiers did the British send over to America to put down the Rebellion of 1776?" In answer to the last question, Mr. Ford replied, "I do not know the exact number of soldiers the British sent over, but I have heard that it was a considerably larger number than ever went back."

Finally, Mr. Ford became tired of this line of questioning and, in reply to a particularly offensive question, he leaned over, pointed his finger at the lawyer who had asked the question, and said, "If I should really *want* to answer the foolish question you have just asked or any of the other questions you have been asking me, let me remind you that I have a row of electric push-buttons on my desk and by pushing the right button, I can summon to my aid people who can answer *any* question I desire to ask concerning the business to which I am devoting most of my efforts. Now, will you kindly tell me, *why* I should clutter up my mind with general knowledge for the purpose of being able to answer questions, when I have people around me who can supply any knowledge I require?"

There certainly was good logic to that reply.

That answer floored the lawyer. Every person in the courtroom realized it was the answer, not of an ignorant man but of a man of *education*. Any person is educated who knows where to get knowledge when needed and how to organize that knowledge into definite plans of action. Through the assistance of his *Master Mind group*, Henry Ford had at his command all the specialized knowledge he needed to enable him to become one of the wealthiest men in America. It was not essential that he have this knowledge in his own mind.

## Andrew Carnegie: Building a steel empire with hired knowledge

Andrew Carnegie stated that he, personally, knew nothing about the technical end of the steel business; moreover, he did not particularly care to know anything about it. The specialized knowledge that he required for the manufacture and marketing of steel he found available through the individual units of his *Master Mind group*.

---

*Any person is educated who knows where to get knowledge when needed and how to organize that knowledge into definite plans of action.*

---

## A salesman who profited from newly acquired specialized knowledge

During an economic downturn, a salesman in a grocery store lost his job due to downsizing. Rather than seek a job in an economy where jobs were scarce, he chose to create a business of his own. Having had some bookkeeping experience, he took a special course in accounting and familiarized himself with all the latest bookkeeping techniques and office equipment. Starting with the grocer for whom he had worked, he made contracts with more than 100 small merchants to keep their books at a very nominal monthly fee. His idea was so practical that he soon found it necessary to set up a portable office in a light delivery truck, which he equipped with modern office equipment. He now has a fleet of these bookkeeping offices "on wheels" and employs a large staff of assistants, providing small merchants with accounting services equal to the best that money can buy at very nominal cost.

Specialized knowledge and imagination were the ingredients that went into this unique and successful business. The beginning of this successful business was an *idea!* When I suggested the plan as a solution of his unemployment problem, he quickly exclaimed, "I like the idea, but I would not know how to turn it into cash." In other words, he complained he would not know how to market his bookkeeping knowledge after he acquired it. This particular obstacle would be solved by another entrepreneur, the leading character of our next success story.

---

**When you choose to pursue riches by selling your specialized knowledge, you may be able to receive a higher price for those services through effective marketing.**

---

### The birth of a clever marketing business

Uncertain of how to effectively market his newly acquired bookkeeping skills, the former grocer salesman (introduced in the previous section) sought the specialized knowledge of a young woman who was clever at hand lettering and could put the story together. Together, they prepared a very attractive describing the advantages of the new system of bookkeeping. The pages were neatly typed and pasted in an ordinary scrapbook, which was used as a sales tool, with which the story of this new business was so effectively told that its owner soon had more accounts than he could handle.

The *idea* here described was born of necessity, to bridge an emergency that had to be covered, but it did not stop by merely serving one person. The woman who created the idea had a keen *imagination* and was *ready* for the idea that presented itself to her. She saw in her newly born brainchild the making of a new profession, one that is destined to render valuable service to thousands of people who need practical guidance in marketing personal services.

Spurred to action by the instantaneous success of her first *"prepared plan to market personal services,"* this energetic woman turned next to the solution of a similar problem for her son who had just finished college but had been totally unable to find a market for his services. The plan she originated for his use was the finest specimen of merchandising of personal services I have ever seen.

When the plan book had been completed, it contained nearly fifty pages of beautifully typed, properly organized information, telling the story of her son's native ability, schooling, personal experiences, and a great variety of other information too extensive for description. The plan book also contained a complete description of the position her son desired, together with a marvelous word picture of the exact plan he would use to fill the position.

The preparation of the plan book required several weeks' labor, during which time its creator sent her son to the public library almost daily to procure data needed in selling his services to best advantage. She sent him also to all the competitors of his prospective employer from which he gathered vital information concerning their business methods. When the plan was finished, it contained more than half a dozen very fine suggestions for the use and benefit of the prospective employer, which were put to good use by the company after it had hired the young man.

One may be inclined to ask, "Why go to all this trouble to secure a job?" The answer is this: When your sole source of income is from providing personal services, extra effort is never wasted in convincing a prospective employer or client that the quality of service you provide is worth more than the standard price paid for such services. The plan prepared by this woman for the benefit of her son helped him get the job for which he applied, at the first interview, at a salary fixed by him. The position did not require the young man to start at the bottom. He began as a junior executive at an executive's salary.

---

*Doing a thing well is never wasted effort!*

---

The woman who prepared the "personal service sales plan" for her son received requests from all parts of the country for her cooperation in preparing similar plans for others who desired to market their personal services for more money. She eventually supervised a staff of expert typists, artists, and writers who had the ability to dramatize the case history so effectively that one's personal services could be marketed for much more money than the prevailing wages for similar services. She was so confident of her ability that she accepted, as the major portion of her fee, a percentage of the increased pay she helped her clients earn. It must not be supposed that her plan merely consisted of clever salesmanship by which she helped men and women to demand and receive more money for the same services they formerly sold for less pay. She looked after the interests of the purchaser as well as the seller of personal services and so prepared her plans that the employer would receive full value for the additional money paid. The method by which she accomplished this astonishing result is a professional secret that she disclosed to no one excepting her own clients.

---

### Avoid the temptation to "start at the bottom and work your way up"

This idea of starting at the bottom and working your way up may appear to be sound, but the major objection to it is that too many of those who begin at the bottom never manage to lift their heads high enough to be seen by *opportunity*, so they remain at the bottom. The outlook from the bottom is not so very bright or encouraging. It has a tendency to stifle ambition. We call it "getting into a rut," which means that we accept our fate because we form the *habit* or daily routine that becomes so entrenched that we stop trying to break it. By starting one or two steps above the bottom, you form the *habit* of looking around, of observing how others get ahead, of seeing *opportunity*, and of embracing it without hesitation.

---

Behind all *ideas* is specialized knowledge. Unfortunately, for those earn a living by selling services, specialized knowledge is more abundant and more easily acquired than *ideas*. Because of this very truth, there is a universal demand and an ever-increasing opportunity for the person capable of helping people sell their personal services advantageously. The woman who prepared the "personal service sales plan" for her son capitalized on this idea, formulated a plan, and combined it with specialized knowledge that yielded riches. The idea is saleable to those seeking new positions calling for managerial or executive ability and those desiring re-arrangement of incomes in their present positions.

## Dan Halpin's unwavering pursuit of success

During his college days, Dan Halpin was student-manager of the famous 1930 National Championship Notre Dame football team, when it was under the direction of the great football coach, Knute Rockne. Perhaps he was inspired by Rockne to aim high and *not mistake temporary defeat for failure*, just as Andrew Carnegie, the great industrial leader, inspired his young business lieutenants to set high goals for themselves. At any rate, young Halpin finished college at a mighty unfavorable time, when the depression had made jobs scarce, so, after a fling at investment banking and motion pictures, he took the first opening with a potential future he could find—selling electrical hearing aids on a commission basis. *Anyone could start in that sort of job, and Halpin knew it*, but it was enough to open the door of opportunity to him.

For almost two years, he continued in a job not to his liking, and he would never have risen above that job if he had not done something about his dissatisfaction. He aimed first at the job of Assistant Sales Manager of his company and got the job. That one step upward placed him high enough above the crowd to enable him to see still greater opportunity. In addition, it placed him where *opportunity could see him.* He made such a fine record selling hearing aids that A. M. Andrews, Chairman of the Board of the Dictograph Products Company, a business competitor of the company for which Halpin worked, wanted to know something about that man Dan Halpin who was taking big sales away from the long established Dictograph Company. He sent for Halpin. When the interview was over, Halpin was the new Sales Manager in charge of Dictograph's Acousticon Division.

Then, to test young Halpin's metal, Mr. Andrews went away to Florida for three months, leaving him to sink or swim in his new job. He did not sink! Knute Rockne's spirit of "All the world loves a winner and has no time for a loser," inspired him to put so much into his job that he was elected Vice-President of the company and General Manager of the Acousticon and Silent Radio Division, a job which most men would be proud to earn through ten years of loyal effort. Halpin turned the trick in little more than six months!

It is difficult to say whether Mr. Andrews or Mr. Halpin is more deserving of eulogy, because both showed evidence of having an abundance of that very rare quality known as *imagination*. Mr. Andrews deserves credit for seeing, in young Halpin, a go-getter of the highest order. Halpin deserves credit for *refusing to compromise with life by accepting and keeping a job he did not want*, and that is one of the major points I am trying to emphasize through this entire philosophy—that we rise to high positions or remain at the bottom *because of conditions we can control if we desire to control them.*

---

### Make success a habit

Both success and failure are largely the results of *habit*! I have not the slightest doubt that Dan Halpin's close association with the greatest football coach America ever knew planted in his mind the same brand of *desire* to excel which made the Notre Dame football team world famous. Truly, there is something to the idea that hero-worship is helpful, provided one worships a *winner*. Halpin tells me that Rockne was one of the world's greatest leaders of men in all history.

---

My belief in the theory that business associations are vital factors, both in failure and in success was demonstrated when my son Blair was negotiating with Dan Halpin for a position. Mr. Halpin offered him a beginning salary of about one half what he could have gotten from a rival company. I brought parental pressure to bear and induced him to accept the place with Mr. Halpin, because I *believe that close association with one who refuses to compromise with circumstances he does not like is an asset that can never be measured in terms of money.*

Successful people decide
and then pursue their goals
with a singularity of purpose.

The value of decisions
depends upon the courage
required to render them.

Procrastination is
symptomatic of
indecisiveness.

# Step 16

# Be Decisive

Analysis of several hundred people who had accumulated fortunes well beyond the million-dollar mark, disclosed the fact that every one of them had the habit of *reaching decisions promptly* and of changing these decisions *slowly*, if and when they were changed. To the contrary, analysis of over 25,000 men and women who had experienced failure disclosed the fact that *lack of decision* was near the head of the list of the 30 major causes of *failure*. People who fail to accumulate money, without exception, have the habit of reaching decisions, *if at all*, very slowly and of changing these decisions quickly and often.

---

*Procrastination*, the opposite of *decision*, is a common enemy that practically everybody must conquer.

---

*Definiteness of decision* always requires courage, sometimes very great courage. People who reach a *definite decision* to procure the particular job and make life pay the price they asks do not stake their life on that decision; they stake their *economic freedom* on that decision. Financial independence, riches, desirable business and professional positions are within reach of only those who *expect, plan,* and *demand* these things. The person, who desires riches in the same spirit that Samuel Adams desired freedom for the Colonies, is sure to accumulate wealth.

## How to become more decisive

"Ready. Aim. Fire." Most people have no trouble with the first two steps. It is that third and final step that trips them up on their path to success; they cannot pull the trigger. They suffer from paralysis by analysis. To become more decisive, try one or more of the following techniques:

- **Commit to a decision date.** Write down the date and time by which you must make the decision and post it where you can see it on a daily basis.
- **Consider the cost of inaction.** Instead of focusing on what you stand to lose if you make a certain decision, consider what you stand to lose if you fail to act.
- **Write down all possible decisions.** When you have a list of decisions from which to choose, making the choice is easier.
- **Limit your research.** Determine what you need to know to make a well-informed decision and obtain only that information. You want to base your decision on facts, but it is very easy to get caught up in never-ending research (paralysis by analysis).
- **Consult your *Master Mind* group.** Individuals who are committed to your best interest may offer viewpoints and additional information that clarify your options.

- **Trust your gut.** Your gut "feeling" is the subconscious mind at work trying to forge the path to what you desire. Do not allow your conscious mind to convince your subconscious of the "impossibility" of a certain idea or plan.
- **Remember that the right choice is not always the perfect choice.** By its very nature, a decision requires you to give up something (the pursuit of the other options) to get what you choose. Knowing that you are at a fork in the road and cannot travel down both paths may be all the impetus you need to make a choice.
- **Decide in steps.** If possible, make your decisions one step at a time. Making a series of smaller decisions may seem less overwhelming than making one big decision. Set milestones to keep yourself on track.

### Make decisiveness a habit

When presented with even the smallest of choices, such as where to dine or what movie to watch, be decisive. Say what *you want* (*desire*) before deferring to someone else or several people in your group. For example, if someone asks where to eat, do not say, "Anything is fine" or "I'm fine with whatever you decide." Instead say something like, "I have a taste for Greek food, but I'm open to hearing other suggestions." Make decisiveness a habit, and you will soon become much better at "pulling the trigger" when facing bigger decisions.

## Tuning out the naysayers

Share your ideas and plans only with the members of your *Master Mind group* (see Step 13), and be certain when assembling this group to choose *only* those who *fully support you* and are *committed to working in your best interest*. If you share your ideas and plans with people outside of your *Master Mind group*, you place your success at risk in two ways:

- Someone may take your idea or execute your plan before you have a chance to. Every person with whom you associate is, like yourself, seeking the opportunity to accumulate money.
- Upon hearing your idea or plan, someone may utter a comment or opinion, perhaps jokingly, that triggers doubt and negative self-talk, which can easily impress itself on your subconscious mind and weaken your desire and enthusiasm. The majority of people who fail to accumulate money sufficient for their needs are, generally, easily influenced by the opinions of others.

---

If you are influenced by the opinions of others when you reach *decisions*, you will not succeed in any undertaking, much less in that of transmuting *your own desire* into money.

---

Keep your eyes and ears wide open and your mouth *closed*, if you wish to acquire the habit of prompt *decision*. Those who talk too much do little else. If you talk more than you listen, you not only deprive yourself of many opportunities to accumulate useful knowledge, but you also disclose your *plans* and *purposes* to people who will take great delight in defeating you, because they envy you.

You have a brain and mind of your own. *Use it* and reach your own decisions. If you need facts or information from other people to enable you to reach decisions, as you probably will in many instances, acquire these facts or secure the information you need quietly, without disclosing your purpose.

---

Let one of your first decisions be to keep a *closed mouth and open ears and eyes.*

---

As a reminder to yourself to follow this advice, copy the following epigram in large letters and place it where you will see it daily.

"*Show it before you tell it.*"

## Stories of decisiveness

Those who reach *decisions* promptly and definitely know what they want and generally get it. The leaders in every walk of life *decide* quickly, and firmly. That is the major reason why they are leaders. The world has the habit of making room for people whose words and actions show that they know where they are going as illustrated in these success stories.

### The decisive and obstinate Henry Ford

One of Henry Ford's most outstanding qualities was his habit of reaching decisions quickly and definitely and changing them slowly. This quality was so pronounced in Mr. Ford that it gave him the reputation of being obstinate. It was this quality that prompted Mr. Ford to continue to manufacture his famous Model "T" (the world's ugliest car), when all of his advisors, and many of the purchasers of the car, were urging him to change it.

Perhaps Mr. Ford delayed too long in making the change, but the other side of the story is that Mr. Ford's firmness of decision yielded a huge fortune before the change in model became necessary. There is but little doubt that Mr. Ford's habit of definiteness of decision assumed the proportion of obstinacy, but this quality is preferable to slowness in reaching decisions and quickness in changing them.

## Freedom or death on a decision

The value of decisions depends upon the courage required to render them. The great decisions, which served as the foundation of civilization, were reached by assuming great risks, which often meant the possibility of death.

---

> The value of decisions depends upon the courage required to render them.

---

Lincoln's decision to issue his famous Proclamation of Emancipation, which gave freedom to the enslaved people of America, was rendered with full understanding that his act would turn thousands of friends and political supporters against him. He knew, too, that the carrying out of that proclamation would mean death to thousands of men on the battlefield. In the end, it cost Lincoln his life. That required courage.

Socrates' decision to drink the cup of poison, rather than compromise in his personal belief was a decision of courage. It turned time ahead a thousand years, and gave to people then unborn, the right to freedom of thought and of speech.

The decision of Gen. Robert E. Lee, when he came to the parting of the way with the Union, and took up the cause of the South, was a decision of courage, for he well knew that it might cost him his own life, that it would surely cost the lives of others.

But, the greatest decision of all time, as far as any American citizen is concerned, was reached in Philadelphia, July 4, 1776, when fifty-six men signed their names to a document, which they well knew would bring freedom to all Americans, or leave every one of the fifty-six hanging from a gallows!

You have heard of this famous document, but you may not have drawn from it the great lesson in personal achievement it so plainly taught.

We all remember the date of this momentous decision, but few of us realize what courage that decision required. We remember our history, as it was taught; we remember dates, and the names of the men who fought; we remember Valley Forge, and Yorktown; we remember George Washington, and Lord Cornwallis. But we know little of the real forces back of these names, dates, and places. We know still less of that intangible *power*, which insured us freedom long before Washington's armies reached Yorktown.

We read the history of the Revolution, and falsely imagine that George Washington was the Father of our Country, that it was he who won our freedom, while the truth is—Washington was only an accessory after the fact, because victory for his armies had been insured long before Lord Cornwallis surrendered. This is not intended to rob Washington of any of the glory he so richly merited. Its purpose, rather, is to give greater attention to the astounding *power* that was the real cause of his victory.

It is nothing short of tragedy that the writers of history have missed, entirely, even the slightest reference to the irresistible *power*, which gave birth and freedom to the nation destined to set up new standards of independence for all the peoples of the earth. I say it is a tragedy, because it is the selfsame *power* that must be used by every individual who surmounts the difficulties of Life, and forces Life to pay the price asked.

Let us briefly review the events that gave birth to this *power*. The story begins with an incident in Boston, March 5, 1770. British soldiers were patrolling the streets, by their presence, openly threatening the citizens. The colonists resented armed men marching in their midst. They began to express their resentment openly, hurling stones as well as epithets, at the marching soldiers, until the commanding officer gave orders, "Fix bayonets. . . . Charge!"

The battle was on. It resulted in the death and injury of many. The incident aroused such resentment that the Provincial Assembly, (made up of prominent colonists), called a meeting for the purpose of taking definite action. Two of the members of that Assembly were John Hancock and Samuel Adams—*long live their names!* They spoke up courageously and declared that a move must be made to eject all British soldiers from Boston.

Remember this—a *decision*, in the minds of two men, might properly be called the beginning of the freedom that we of the United States now enjoy. Remember, too, that the *decision* of these two men called for *faith* and *courage*, because it was dangerous.

Before the Assembly adjourned, Samuel Adams was appointed to call on the Governor of the Province, Hutchinson and demand the withdrawal of the British troops.

The request was granted, the troops were removed from Boston, but the incident was not closed. It had caused a situation destined to change the entire trend of civilization. Strange, is it not, how the great changes, such as the American Revolution and many wars, often have their beginnings in circumstances which seem unimportant? It is interesting, also, to observe that these important changes usually begin in the form of a *definite decision* in the minds of a relatively small number of people. Few of us know the history of our country well enough to realize that John Hancock, Samuel Adams, and Richard Henry Lee (of the Province of Virginia) were the real Fathers of our Country.

Richard Henry Lee became an important factor in this story by reason of the fact that he and Samuel Adams communicated frequently (by correspondence), sharing freely their fears and their hopes concerning the welfare of the people of their Provinces. From this practice, Adams conceived the idea that a mutual exchange of letters between the thirteen Colonies might help to bring about the coordination of effort so badly needed in connection with the solution of their problems. Two years after the clash with the soldiers in Boston (March 1772), Adams presented this idea to the Assembly, in the form of a motion that a Correspondence Committee be established among the Colonies, with definitely appointed correspondents in each Colony, "for the purpose of friendly cooperation for the betterment of the Colonies of British America."

Mark well this incident! It was the beginning of the organization of the far-flung *power* destined to give freedom to you and me. The *Master Mind* had already been organized. It consisted of Adams, Lee, and Hancock. The Committee of Correspondence was organized. Observe that this move provided the way for increasing the power of the Master Mind by adding to it men from all the Colonies. Take notice that this procedure constituted the first *organized planning* of the disgruntled Colonists.

In union there is strength! The citizens of the Colonies had been waging disorganized warfare against the British soldiers, through incidents similar to the Boston riot, but nothing of benefit had been accomplished. Their individual grievances had not been consolidated under one *Master Mind*. No group of individuals had put their hearts, minds, souls, and bodies together in one definite *decision* to settle their difficulty with the British once and for all, until Adams, Hancock, and Lee got together.

Meanwhile, the British were not idle. They, too, were doing some *planning* and *Master-Minding* on their own account, with the advantage of having money and organized soldiery.

The Crown appointed Gage to supplant Hutchinson as the Governor of Massachusetts. One of the new Governor's first acts was to send a messenger to call on Samuel Adams for the purpose of endeavoring to stop his opposition—by *fear*.

We can best understand the spirit of what happened by quoting the conversation between Col. Fenton, (the messenger sent by Gage), and Adams.

Col. Fenton presented the carrot and the stick:

> I have been authorized by Governor Gage, to assure you, Mr. Adams, that the Governor has been empowered to

confer upon you such benefits as would be satisfactory [carrot], upon the condition that you engage to cease in your opposition to the measures of the government. It is the Governor's advice to you, Sir, not to incur the further displeasure of his majesty. Your conduct has been such as makes you liable to penalties of an Act of Henry VIII, by which persons can be sent to England for trial for treason, or misprision of treason, at the discretion of a governor of a province [stick]. But, *by changing your political course*, you will not only receive great personal advantages, but you will make your peace with the King.

Samuel Adams had the choice of two *decisions*. He could cease his opposition and receive personal bribes, or he could *continue and run the risk of being hanged!*

Clearly, the time had come when Adams was forced to reach instantly a *decision* that could have cost his life. The majority of people would have found it difficult to reach such a decision. The majority would have sent back an evasive reply, but not Adams! He insisted upon Col. Fenton's word of honor that the Colonel would deliver to the Governor the answer exactly as Adams would give it to him.

Adams' answer:

Then you may tell Governor Gage that I trust I have long since made my peace with the King of Kings. No personal consideration shall induce me to abandon the righteous cause of my Country. And, *tell Governor Gage it is the advice of Samuel Adams to him*, no longer to insult the feelings of an exasperated people.

Comment as to the character of this man seems unnecessary. It must be obvious to all who read this astounding message that its sender possessed loyalty of the highest order. This is important. (Racketeers and dishonest politicians have prostituted the honor for which such men as Adams died.)

When Governor Gage received Adams' caustic reply, he flew into a rage and issued a proclamation which read:

> I do, hereby, in his majesty's name, offer and promise his most gracious pardon to all persons who shall forthwith lay down their arms and return to the duties of peaceable subjects, excepting only from the benefit of such pardon, *Samuel Adams and John Hancock*, whose offences are of too flagitious a nature to admit of any other consideration but that of condign punishment.

As one might say, in modern slang, Adams and Hancock were "on the spot!" The threat of the irate Governor forced the two men to reach another decision, equally as dangerous. They hurriedly called a secret meeting of their staunchest followers. (Here the *Master Mind* began to take on momentum). After the meeting had been called to order, Adams locked the door, placed the key in his pocket, and informed all present that it was imperative that a Congress of the Colonists be organized and that *no man should leave the room until the decision for such a Congress had been reached.*

Great excitement followed. Some weighed the possible consequences of such radicalism. (Fear). Some expressed grave doubt as to the Wisdom of so definite a decision in defiance of the Crown. Locked in that room were *two men* immune to

Fear, blind to the possibility of Failure: Hancock and Adams. Through the influence of their minds, the others were induced to agree that, through the Correspondence Committee, arrangements should be made for a meeting of the First Continental Congress to be held in Philadelphia, September 5, 1774.

Remember this date. It is more important than July 4, 1776. If there had been no *decision* to hold a Continental Congress, there could have been no signing of the Declaration of Independence.

Before the first meeting of the new Congress, another leader, in a different section of the country was deep in the throes of publishing a "Summary View of the Rights of British America." He was Thomas Jefferson, of the Province of Virginia, whose relationship to Lord Dunmore (representative of the Crown in Virginia) was as strained as that of Hancock and Adams with their Governor.

Shortly after his famous Summary of Rights was published, Jefferson was informed that he was subject to prosecution for high treason against his majesty's government. Inspired by the threat, one of Jefferson's colleagues, Patrick Henry, boldly spoke his mind, concluding his remarks with a sentence that shall remain forever a classic, "If this be treason, then make the most of it."

It was such men as these who, without power, without authority, without military strength, without money, sat in solemn consideration of the destiny of the colonies, beginning at the opening of the First Continental Congress and continuing at intervals for two years until, on June 7, 1776, Richard Henry Lee arose, addressed the Chair, and to the startled Assembly made this motion:

> Gentlemen, I make the motion that these United Colonies are, and of right ought to be free and independent states, that they be absolved from all allegiance to the British Crown, and that all political connection between them and the state of Great Britain is, and ought to be totally dissolved.

Lee's astounding motion was discussed fervently and at such length that he began to lose patience. Finally, after days of argument, he again took the floor and declared, in a clear, firm voice:

> Mr. President, we have discussed this issue for days. It is the only course for us to follow. Why, then Sir, do we longer delay? Why still deliberate? Let this happy day give birth to an American Republic. Let her arise, not to devastate and to conquer, but to reestablish the reign of peace, and of law. The eyes of Europe are fixed upon us. She demands of us a living example of freedom that may exhibit a contrast, in the felicity of the citizen, to the ever increasing tyranny.

Before his motion was finally voted upon, Lee was called back to Virginia because of serious family illness, but before leaving he placed his cause in the hands of his friend, Thomas Jefferson, who promised to fight until favorable action was taken. Shortly thereafter, the President of the Congress (Hancock) appointed Jefferson as Chairman of a Committee to draw up a Declaration of Independence.

Long and hard the Committee labored on a document which would mean, when accepted by the Congress, that *every man who signed it would be signing his own death warrant* should the Colonies lose in the fight with Great Britain, which was sure to follow.

The document was drawn, and on June 28 the original draft was read before the Congress. For several days it was discussed, altered, and made ready. On July 4, 1776, Thomas Jefferson stood before the Assembly and fearlessly read the most momentous *decision* ever placed upon paper:

> When in the course of human events it is necessary for one people to dissolve the political bands which have connected them with another, and to assume, among the powers of the earth, the separate and equal station to which the laws of Nature, and of Nature's God entitle them, a decent respect to the opinions of mankind requires that they should declare the causes which impel them to the separation. . . .

When Jefferson finished, the document was voted upon, accepted, and signed by the fifty-six men, every one staking his own life upon his *decision* to write his name. By that *decision* came into existence a nation destined to bring to mankind forever the privilege of making *decisions*.

By decisions made in a similar spirit of Faith, and only by such decisions, can men solve their personal problems and win for themselves high estates of material and spiritual wealth. Let us not forget this!

Analyze the events that led to the Declaration of Independence and be convinced that this nation, which now holds a position of commanding respect and power among all nations of the world, was born of a *decision* created by a *Master Mind*, consisting of fifty-six men. Note well the fact that it was their *decision* that ensured the success of Washington's armies, because the spirit of that decision was in the heart of every soldier who fought with him and served as a spiritual power that recognizes no such thing as *failure*.

Note, also, (with great personal benefit), that the *power* that gave this nation its freedom, is the self-same power that must be used by every individual who becomes self-determining. This *power* is made up of the principles described in this book. It will not be difficult to detect, in the story of the Declaration of Independence, at least six of these principles; *desire, decision, faith, persistence, the Master Mind*, and *organized planning*.

## Fred Smith decides to make FEDEX a success

A modern example of a person who displayed courage in making decisions is Fred Smith, the founder of Federal Express (FEDEX).

When Smith was a student in an economics class at Yale University, his professor stated that airfreight was the wave of the future and would be the primary source of revenue for the airlines.

Smith wrote a paper disagreeing. His argument was that the passenger route patterns that were the primary airline routes were wrong for freight. He noted that because costs would not come down with volume, the only way airfreight could be profitable was through a whole new system that would reach out to smaller cities as well as big ones and be designed for packages, not people. The professor considered this entirely unfeasible and gave Smith's paper a low grade.

Smith's concept was to start an all-freight airline that would fly primarily at night when the airports weren't congested. It would carry small, high-priority packages when speed of delivery was more important than cost. It would bring all the packages to a central point (He chose his home town—Memphis) where, through a specially designed computer program, the packages would be sorted, dispersed, and loaded on airplanes that were flown to the ultimate destinations. By consolidating all shipments to smaller cities, it would enable the company to fly full planeloads to cities all over the country and eventually the world. Smith believed that venture capitalists would be interested and excited about this innovative idea. But, to his shock, little interest was developed in the financial community.

This did not stop Smith. Because of his enthusiasm for the project and the courage of his convictions, he raised $91 million to finance his untested idea.

At this point, the competing carriers realized that Smith's concept was a potential threat to their industry. The major airlines tried to forestall this new competition by lobbying the Civil Aeronautics Board to refuse Smith the necessary permission. Smith's team found a loophole in the law. Planes with a payload under 7,500 pounds did not need CAB permission to operate.

Smith went ahead and assembled a fleet of small jets. He began construction of his main facility at Memphis and began servicing 75 airports. FEDEX would pick up packages at airports all over the country and fly them to Memphis, where they were sorted out and processed for immediate reshipment to other cities. Once unloaded, FEDEX trucks delivered them to their destinations. Smith set a goal to get all packages to their destinations within 24 hours of its pick-up—and this goal was almost always met.

Despite the hard work and efforts of the company, the first few years were financial disasters. Losses amounted to millions of dollars. The investors were seriously concerned. FEDEX was falling far short of Smith's projections.

Despite the losses—which the investors blamed on Smith—and even talk of removing him and taking over the company. Smith did not lose faith. His courage never faltered. He hired experts (his *Master Mind*) and worked day and night with them to solve operational problems. This resulted in FEDEX's revenues reaching $75 million in the next fiscal year with a profit of $3.6 million.

Despite competition from faxes that virtually eliminated use of FEDEX for letters and documents and competition from other airfreight companies and the United States Postal Service, which offered overnight service at a much lower price, Smith's continued innovation and dedication to continuous improvement have kept FEDEX as the number one carrier in its field.

*Persist:* To forge ahead despite opposition, misfortune, and criticism.

Persistence is to character what carbon is to steel.

Every failure brings with it the seed of an equivalent advantage.

# Step 17

# Be Persistent

*Persistence* is an essential factor for transmuting *desire* into its monetary equivalent, and the basis of persistence is *willpower*. Willpower and desire, when properly combined, make an invincible pair.

*Persistence* is a state of mind, therefore it can be cultivated. Like all states of mind, persistence is based upon definite causes, among them these:

- **Definiteness of purpose:** Knowing what you want or want to accomplish is the first and, perhaps, the most important step toward developing persistence. A strong motive forces you to surmount many difficulties.
- **Desire:** It is comparatively easy to acquire and maintain persistence in pursuing the object of intense desire.
- **Faith:** Belief in your ability to carry out a plan encourages you to follow the plan through with persistence. (See Step 8 for more about faith.)

- **Definiteness of plans:** Organized plans, even though they may be weak and entirely impractical, encourage persistence.
- **Accurate knowledge:** Knowing that one's plans are sound, based upon experience or observation, encourages persistence; guessing instead of knowing destroys persistence.
- **Cooperation:** Sympathy, understanding, and harmonious cooperation with others tend to develop persistence.
- **Willpower:** The habit of concentrating one's thoughts upon the building of plans for the attainment of a definite purpose leads to persistence.
- **Habit:** Persistence is the direct result of habit. The mind absorbs and becomes a part of the daily experiences upon which it feeds. Fear, the worst of all enemies, can be effectively cured by forced repetition of acts of courage. Everyone who has seen active service in war knows this.

Ask the first hundred people you meet what they want most in life, and ninety eight of them will not be able to tell you. If you press them for an answer, some will say *security,* many will say *money,* a few will say *happiness,* others will say *fame and power,* and still others will say *social recognition, ease in living, ability to sing, dance,* or *write,* but none of them will be able to define these terms or give the slightest indication of a *plan* by which they hope to attain these vaguely expressed wishes.

> Riches do not respond to wishes.
> They respond only to definite *desires*, executed
> according to definite *plans* with *persistence*.

## Distinguish between persistence and ruthlessness

People who accumulate great fortunes are often misperceived as cold-blooded or ruthless when they are merely persistent. What they have is willpower mixed with persistence and placed behind their desires to ensure the attainment of their objectives. "Ruthlessness" involves a lack of pity or compassion, the trampling of other people's interests in pursuit of one's own. Although some wealthy individuals truly are ruthless, the vast majority of those who achieve and maintain wealth do so without the intention of unfairly exploiting others.

Henry Ford was often misconstrued as being ruthless and cold-blooded. This misconception grew out of Ford's habit of following through in all of his plans with *persistence*.

The majority of people are ready to throw their aims and purposes overboard and give up at the first sign of opposition or misfortune. A few carry on *despite* all opposition, until they attain their goal. These few are the Fords, Carnegies, Rockefellers, and Edisons.

> There may be no heroic connotation
> to the word "persistence," but the quality
> is to character what carbon is to steel.

## Check yourself for symptoms of lack of persistence

Take inventory of yourself and determine in what particular, if any, you are lacking in this essential quality of *persistence*. Measure yourself courageously, point by point, and see how many of the sixteen factors of persistence you lack. The analysis may lead to discoveries that will give you a new grip on yourself.

Here you will find the real enemies that stand between you and noteworthy achievement—not only the symptoms indicating weakness of *persistence*, but also the deeply seated subconscious causes of this weakness. Study the list carefully, and face yourself squarely *if you really wish to know who you are and what you are capable of doing*. These are the weaknesses that must be overcome by all who accumulate riches:

- *Fear of criticism*, failure to create plans and to put them into action, because of what other people will think, do, or say. This enemy belongs at the head of the list, because it generally exists in one's subconscious mind, where its presence is not recognized. (For more about overcoming the six basic fears that stand in the way of success, see Step 3.)
- Failure to recognize and to clearly define exactly what you want.
- Procrastination, with or without cause. (Usually backed up with a formidable array of excuses).
- Lack of interest in acquiring specialized knowledge.

- Indecision, the habit of "passing the buck" on all occasions, instead of facing issues squarely (also backed by excuses).
- The habit of relying upon excuses instead of creating definite plans for the solution of problems.
- Self-satisfaction. There is but little remedy for this affliction and no hope for those who suffer from it.
- Indifference, usually reflected in one's readiness to compromise on all occasions, rather than meet opposition and fight it.
- The habit of blaming others for one's mistakes and accepting unfavorable circumstances as being unavoidable.
- *Weakness of desire*, due to neglect in the choice of *motives* that impel action.
- Willingness, even eagerness, to quit at the first sign of defeat, a characteristic that often arises from one or more of the six basic fears, as described in Step 3.
- Lack of *organized plans* in writing where they may be analyzed.
- The habit of neglecting to move on ideas or to grasp opportunity when it presents itself.
- *Wishing* instead of *willing*.
- The habit of compromising with *poverty* instead of aiming at riches—a general absence of ambition to *be*, to *do*, and to *own*.
- Searching for all the short-cuts to riches, trying to *get* without *giving* a fair equivalent, usually reflected in the habit of gambling or endeavoring to drive "sharp" bargains.

---

### The acid test for persistence

Continue to read through to the end of this chapter, then go back to Step 5, "Develop a Burning Desire," and perform the six steps to transmute desire to riches. The eagerness with which you follow these instructions will indicate clearly how much or how little you really *desire* to accumulate money. If you find that you are indifferent, you may be sure that you have not yet acquired the *money consciousness* which you must possess before you can be sure of accumulating a fortune.

---

## Develop and strengthen your persistence

There are four simple steps that lead to the habit of *persistence*. They call for no great amount of intelligence, no particular amount of education, and but little time or effort. The necessary steps are:

1. **Nurture your desire until you have a burning desire for its fulfillment.** The ease with which lack of persistence may be conquered depends upon the *intensity of one's desire*. Follow the instructions in Step 6 on autosuggestion to impress upon your mind a clear picture of the object of your *desire*.
2. **Formulate a definite plan to fulfill your desire.** A plan is a bridge from what you imagine to its physical manifestation, reinforcing your faith in ultimately receiving that which you desire. See Step 14 for more about organized planning.

# Be Persistent 335

3. **Execute your plan with continuous action.** You may find it necessary to "snap" out of your mental inertia by moving slowly at first, then increasing your speed, until you gain complete control over your will. Be *persistent* no matter how slowly you may, at first, have to move. *With persistence will come success.*
4. **Close your mind tightly against all negative and discouraging influences, including negative suggestions of relatives, friends and acquaintances.** Discouraging influences interject doubt which is the opposite of faith. See Step 16, "Be Decisive," for guidance on tuning out the naysayers.
5. **Forge a friendly alliance with one or more persons who will encourage you to follow through with both plan and purpose.** If you select your *Master Mind group* with care, you will have in it, at least one person who will aid you in the development of *persistence*. Turn to Chapter 13 for instructions on assembling your *Master Mind group*.

---

> Weak desires bring weak results, just as a small amount of fire makes a small amount of heat.

---

These five steps are essential for success in all walks of life. The entire purpose of the thirteen principles of this philosophy is to enable one to adopt these five steps as a matter of *habit*.

- These are the steps by which you may control your economic destiny.
- They lead to freedom and independence of thought.
- They lead to riches, in small or great quantities.
- They lead the way to power, fame, and worldly recognition.
- They guarantee favorable opportunities.

- They convert dreams into physical realities.
- They lead to the mastery over fear, discouragement, and indifference.

There is a magnificent reward for all who learn to take these five steps. It is the privilege of writing one's own ticket and of making Life yield whatever price is asked.

---

*There is no substitute for persistence!*
It cannot be supplanted by any other quality! Remember this, and it will hearten you, in the beginning, when the going may seem difficult and slow.

---

## Reap the rewards of persistence

Those who have cultivated the *habit* of persistence seem to enjoy insurance against failure. No matter how many times they are defeated, they finally arrive up toward the top of the ladder. Sometimes it appears that there is a hidden Guide whose duty is to test people through all sorts of discouraging experiences. Those who pick themselves up after defeat and keep on trying arrive, and the world cries, "Bravo! I knew you could do it!" The hidden Guide lets no one enjoy great achievement without passing the *persistence test*. Those who can't pass it simply do not make the grade.

---

Some people who have accumulated great fortunes did so out of *necessity*, because they were so closely driven by circumstances that they had to become persistent.

---

Those who pass the test are bountifully rewarded for their *persistence*. They receive, as their compensation, whatever goal they are pursuing. That is not all! They receive something infinitely more important than material compensation—the knowledge that *"every failure brings with it the seed of an equivalent advantage."*

There are exceptions to this rule; a few people know from experience the soundness of persistence. They are the ones who have not accepted defeat as being anything more than temporary. They are the ones whose *desires* are so *persistently applied* that defeat is finally changed into victory. We who stand on the sidelines of Life see the overwhelmingly large number who go down in defeat, never to rise again. We see the few who take the punishment of defeat as an urge to greater effort. These, fortunately, never learn to accept Life's reverse gear. But what we *do not see*, what most of us never suspect of existing, is the silent but irresistible *power* which comes to the rescue of those who fight on in the face of discouragement. If we speak of this power at all we call it *persistence,* and let it go at that. One thing we all know, if one does not possess *persistence*, one does not achieve noteworthy success in any calling.

---

A silent but irresistible *power* comes to the rescue of those who fight on in the face of discouragement.

---

## Success stories: Persistence pays

What mystical power does *persistence* give people the capacity to master difficulties? Does the quality of *persistence* set up in one's mind some form of spiritual, mental or chemical activity that gives one access to supernatural forces? Does Infinite Intelligence throw itself on the side of the person who still fights on, after the battle has been lost, with the whole world on the opposing side?

These and many other similar questions have arisen in my mind as I have observed men like Henry Ford, who started from scratch and built an Industrial Empire of huge proportions with little else in the way of a beginning but *persistence*. And Thomas A. Edison, who, with less than three months of schooling, became the world's leading inventor and converted *persistence* into the talking machine, the moving picture machine, and the incandescent lightbulb, to say nothing of more than 50 other useful inventions.

I had the happy privilege of analyzing both Mr. Edison and Mr. Ford, year by year, over a long period of years, and therefore, the opportunity to study them at close range, so I speak from actual knowledge when I say that I found no quality save *persistence*, in either of them, that even remotely suggested the major source of their stupendous achievements.

As one makes an impartial study of successful people, one is drawn to the inevitable conclusion that *persistence*, concentration of effort, and *definiteness of purpose*, were the major sources of their achievements.

---

There may be no heroic connotation
to the word "persistence," but the quality
is to character what carbon is to steel.

---

## Bruce Lee

A good example of the power of persistence is show business. From all over the world people have come to Hollywood, seeking fame, fortune, power, love, or whatever it is that human beings call success. Once in a great while someone steps out from the long procession of seekers, and the world hears that another person has mastered Hollywood. But Hollywood is not easily nor quickly conquered. It acknowledges talent, recognizes genius, and pays off in money only after one has refused to *quit*. The secret is always inseparably attached to one word, *persistence!*

Bruce Lee, the actor who made America conscious of the Asian martial arts, might have been long ago forgotten were it not for his persistence is reaching for movie stardom.

Lee arrived in the U. S. from China with nothing but a dream and the capacity for hard work.

During his youth he studied and mastered kung-fu and later became a teacher of this art. However, his real goal was to be an actor. He obtained minor roles in some movies and TV programs, but he felt his great break came when he learned that the producers of a new television series called "Kung Fu" were looking for an actor who knew martial arts for the starring role in this program. His screen test was successful and he looked forward to being given the role, but to his great disappointment, another actor, David Carradine, was chosen.

Disillusioned, he was ready to give up acting and go back to teaching. When members of the Asian community heard of this, he was deluged with letters asking him not to give up. Soon the word spread to movie fans of all races, and Lee made up his mind to keep seeking new roles.

He never gave up. He took roles in several movies and his reputation as an actor and proponent of the martial arts made his name a household word throughout the world and took the study of the martial arts from being limited to Asian countries to becoming universally respected.

Although he died at the age of 32 of a cerebral hemorrhage, his fame has lived on. Bruce Lee is still remembered and admired by fans—many of whom were not even born when he made his movies. His TV series and early movies have been made into videos and are still highly popular all over the world.

## Howard Schultz, the Starbucks man

A good example of determination and persistence is Howard Schultz, the "Starbucks man." It takes a person with vision, fortitude, and unswerving confidence to make a new concept succeed.

Schultz was hired to manage retail sales and marketing for a small coffee distributor who had a few retail outlets in Seattle. He was 29 and just married. He and his wife left their home in New York City to accept this new job.

About a year later, Schultz visited Italy on a buying trip. As he wandered around Milan, he noticed how important coffee was to the Italian culture. Typically, the workday starts with a cup of rich coffee at a coffee bar. After work, friends and colleague once again meet at the coffee bar for a leisurely stop before heading home. It is a center of Italian social life. Schultz visualized this transferred to America. It had never been done. But he felt it could work because of the high quality of Starbucks coffee.

It became Schultz's obsession. He was determined to build a national chain of cafés based on the Italian coffee bar, but the

Starbuck's owners were reluctant. They were in the wholesale coffee bean business; the restaurants they owned were only a small part of their operation.

To implement his goal, Schultz left Starbucks and planned a new company. In 1986, Schultz opened his first coffee bar in Seattle. It was an immediate success. Schultz soon opened another in Seattle and a third in Vancouver. The following year he bought the Starbucks Company and adopted its name for his enterprise.

Schultz believes that the quality of Starbucks will one day alter how everyday Americans conduct their lives. If Schultz has his way, a cup of Starbucks will become a basic part of American culture. His concept has paid off. Starbucks's sales have increased every year since 1988.

Schultz envisioned hundreds of Starbucks coffee shops across America, shops that business people would stop at on their way to work and come to after work to relax. Shoppers would stop for a pick-me-up. Young people would meet their dates over coffee rather than cocktails. Families would come for refreshment before or after the movies.

Starbucks incurred losses for three straight years—more than $1 million in 1989 alone, but Schultz never gave up. He had a firm conviction that this was the way to build a company and that the losses would soon turn into profits.

Once his Seattle stores were profitable, Starbucks spread slowly into other cities—Vancouver, Portland, Los Angeles, Denver, and Chicago, and later to the eastern cities and overseas. Starbucks has become a household name all over the world and an exemplar of American marketing ingenuity. And it has made Howard Schultz one of the world's richest people.

## Domino's Pizza

Many people believe that material success is the result of favorable "breaks." There is an element of ground for the belief, but those depending entirely upon luck, are nearly always disappointed, because they overlook another important factor that must be present before one can be sure of success. It is the knowledge with which favorable "breaks" can be made to order.

Let's look at Tom Monaghan, who created and grew Domino's Pizzas from a one-store pizza parlor to a chain of several thousand home-delivery outlets over a period of about 30 years. In 1989, he decided to sell his hugely successful company to concentrate instead on doing philanthropic work.

However, his plan did not work out. After two and a half years, the company that purchased the chain almost drove it into bankruptcy so Monaghan came back.

It took much hard work and persistence to first rebuild and then expand the organization. Monaghan had developed the necessary determination early in his life. He had overcame a childhood of deprivation, poverty and abuse to become a great entrepreneur. Now once again he mobilized all his efforts to not only return Domino's to its original prominence but to expand it to 6000 stores—of which 1100 are in countries other than the United States.

Once the chain was back on its feet, Monaghan faced a new and serious challenge. Domino's built its major promotion on their guarantee of fast delivery. They guaranteed the customer would get their pizza within 30 minutes.

This led to a series of law suits from people who claimed injury from accidents caused by Domino's delivery drivers who were speeding to make the 30-minute deadline. The family of a woman allegedly killed by a Domino's driver in Indiana was awarded $3 million. The final blow came when another woman was awarded $78 million. After that Domino's dropped the 30-minute guarantee.

Despite this financial catastrophe, Monaghan refused to give up. He plowed more money, time and energy into the company and brought it back once again. By his persistence and positive attitude he forged ahead and inspired his team with the winning spirit that has made Domino's number one in its industry.

www.ingramcontent.com/pod-product-compliance
Lightning Source LLC
Chambersburg PA
CBHW052011070526
44584CB00016B/1708